A SILENT MAN

The Dunham/McGlincy Murders

edited by

Douglas MacGowan

Published by:

The Campbell Historical Museum & Ainsley House Foundation

Dedicated to Marian, who fed the peacocks with me.

Editor's Introduction

This book is not a whodunnit. From the first moments, the identity of the murderer was known due to the crime being witnessed by two people.

A Silent Man chronicles a crime that was infamous for many years in Santa Clara County, California, during the bridge between the 19th and 20th centuries. I have edited the book to, I hope, be unique in an interesting way. Except for a few brief clarification notes, the book is told entirely by contemporary newspaper articles as the story of the crime and the subsequent investigation unfolded. This gives the reader an opportunity to see the facts and theories exactly as they were presented to the avidly curious residents of the area. Readers will discover the facts of the crime itself, of the backgrounds of the victims and the murderer, and of the actions of the law officers in the same sequence in which they were revealed to the population of Santa Clara County.

I have liberally edited the articles for clarification and to remove repetitions and unnecessary text. During the investigation there were countless articles which consisted of the cycle of law officers following up a possible lead only to return back to Square One and then to go out on the next unsuccessful hunt for the murderer.

And so we begin.

Newspaper: *San Jose Mercury*
Date: May 7, 1896

Birth Announcements

DUNHAM—At Campbell, May 4, 1896, to Mr. and Mrs. J. C. Dunham, a son.

Newspaper: *Campbell Weekly Visitor*
Date: May 16, 1896

Colonel McGlincy attended an IOOF (Independent Order of Odd Fellows) convention in San Francisco the past week.

Newspaper: *Campbell Weekly Visitor*
Date: May 23, 1896

The Cambrian Literary Society met at the usual hour on last Saturday evening with a fair attendance. The minutes of the last meeting were read and approved. The program of the evening was as follows: recitation, Ruth Drake; Song, Preat Ross; guitar solo James Wells; reading of the Society paper, Miss Cora Dean.

Newspaper: *Campbell Weekly Visitor*
Date: May 23, 1896

James Wells and Loyd Buffington were given a terrible fall on Sunday morning last by the breaking of the front fork of the tandem bicycle which they were riding at 2:30 gait. The accident occurred on the Los Gatos and Santa Clara road near the Winchester place. As the wheel gave way, both the riders were thrown to the gravel road with great force. James Wells was picked up unconscious and carried into a house nearby and the doctor sent for. He remained unconscious for about an hour when he revived somewhat and was taken to his home south of town. His injuries did not prove serious, however, and

1

he was out again on Tuesday. Both the boys were badly bruised and scratched up about the head and face and the fact that they escaped without fatal consequences seems a miracle.

Newspaper: *San Jose Mercury*
Date: May 27, 1896

A tragedy unparalleled in the history of Santa Clara County was enacted last night at 12:00, resulting in the death of six people, and blotting out the existence of the entire family of Colonel Richard P. McGlincy, one of the most prominent residents in the Campbell District, six miles southwest of San Jose. Colonel McGlincy, Mrs. McGlincy, her son and daughter, a hired girl and a hired man were the victims of the awful tragedy enacted by a son-in-law of Mrs. McGlincy named James Dunham. There is only a baby, Dunham's child, survivor of the family. One hired man narrowly escaped the fate of the others.

The McGlincy home is located one mile south of Campbell Station, and was the scene of the murders.

The only witnesses to the deeds were a hired man who viewed the killing of the father, and a young man named Ross, son of a neighbor, the former viewing from a window in the barn and the latter from behind the barn.

It was nearly 8:00 this morning before communication could be established between San Jose to persons in any way familiar with the murder.

It is thought that the three women were killed first, and then the fiend waited for the men to march in to their doom.

When found, the young wife of Dunham was lying upon her bed, dead. Her death was evidently accomplished by choking.

By the side of the bed lay the hired girl, known as Minnie Shesler. She was also dead. Her home is in San Jose on Willow Street, near Delmas Avenue.

James K. Wells, Mrs. McGlincy's son, was found in the sitting room on the floor, and his clothes were afire, having been ignited from the pistol that ended his life. Here there were evidences of an awful struggle, a mighty fight for his life.

Colonel McGlincy, on realizing the seriousness of the situation, ran from the house terror-stricken, screaming murder with all the power of voice and crying for help.

His refuge was the cabin occupied by hired men, and he ran in there for protection.

Close behind him came Dunham, pistol in hand. Dunham demanded McGlincy to come out. He waited but a short time and then began firing bullets through the door.

The hired man, Robert Briscoe, soon followed Colonel McGlincy from the cabin and met the same fate. He exerted all his strength and managed to crawl about 50 yards back of the cabin, and there dying from a bullet through his heart.

The other hired man would have undoubtedly met death had he not been in the barn. He saw the killing of the two men from the barn window.

In the killing of six persons, Dunham employed various methods.

His wife, with whom he had apparently lived happily, had been tortured with strangulation, and down her throat were crowded clothes in order to make certain that she could not revive and recover her breath. By her side lay her baby, sleeping peacefully, and could not cause those who viewed the scene of death to wonder why the fiend had exercised the slightest mercy.

Minnie Shesler, the hired girl, doubtless made a more vigorous struggle for her life than the wife of Dunham. She was choked, and clothing had been jammed down her throat, and she lay in a pool of her own blood.

Mrs. McGlincy was found in her own room, and was the subject of Dunham's most brutal work.

She'd been beaten over the head with a hatchet, and her skull was thus crushed in.

After completing his record of murder, Dunham took a horse from the barn and without taking time to saddle left the place.

Dunham was last seen about 1:00 by a young man at the intersection of Campbell Avenue and the Los Gatos Road. He had secured a saddle and was evidently counting on a long ride.

George Schaible, the hired man who returned from Campbell with Colonel McGlincy, was interviewed by a Mercury reporter. "When Mr. McGlincy and I got home," said Schaible, "he told me to go up in the loft and pitch down some hay. He then started toward the house. While I was up in the loft, I heard shots being fired and I looked out.

"I saw Colonel McGlincy running towards the cabin shouting for help, and Dunham was following him up shooting at him. And I heard McGlincy say 'Don't shoot me anymore, I got two bullets in my body now.'"

As he fell, I stepped back as I was afraid he would see me and kill me, too. I heard more shots fired, and when I looked out again Dunham was riding the way down the road."

Colonel McGlincy was a native of Virginia, aged 54 years. He was in the Confederate service during the war of the rebellion. Before coming to California he was a newspaper writer. At the world's fair, Chicago, he had charge of the Santa Clara county exhibit.

Newspaper: *Sacramento Bee*
Date: May 27, 1896

SAN JOSE. The most horrible crime in the history of the county was perpetrated at Campbell, a small place about 6 miles southwest of this city this morning. Colonel R. P. McGlincy and his wife; their daughter, Mrs. James Dunham; James Wells, a son of Mrs. McGlincy; a hired woman, Minnie Shesler; and a hired man, James Briscoe, were killed by James Dunham, son-in-law of Colonel McGlincy, who made his escape.

About midnight a neighbor by the name of Page heard the report of shots in the direction of the McGlincy home. Almost immediately thereafter there came the sound of galloping hoofs on the county road. Hurriedly dressing, Page proceeded to the home of the McGlincy's, and was horrified to find the body of Mr. McGlincy lying in an outhouse in a pool of blood.

Entering the main house, he found the bodies of James Wells, who had been shot; Mrs. McGlincy and her daughter, who had been stabbed to death by the a single assassin; and the hired man and girl, who had been hacked to death with a hatchet.

The interior of the rooms where the bodies of the victims lay were bespattered with blood, and there was every evidence to show that the dead had made a desperate struggle for their lives.

Page, finding that all were beyond help, proceeded at once to notify the authorities in this city, and word was immediately telephoned to officers in all parts of the county to be on the lookout for the assassin. A large number of officers and men left immediately for the scene of the murder.

The murdered family was one of the best known in the valley, members of the San Jose Grange, and prominently identified with the fruit business.

The McGlincy home is in the midst of what is acknowledged to be the most beautiful and prosperous section of Santa Clara County, a region of orchard homes.

Campbell is known as the prohibition town of Santa Clara County, and is largely settled by the prosperous easterners, such as have built up Pasadena, Redlands, Pomona, and other towns in Southern California.

At 3:00 AM one of the officers returned to the city from the scene, and in an interview said: "The scene at the McGlincy home is one fearful almost beyond the power of description.

"In the reception room was found the body of Wells. Evidently a terrible struggle had taken place between Wells and the assassin. Wells was shot two or three times, blood was splashed all over the room, and before leaving his victim the assassin had fired his clothing.

"In the reception room, adjoining, no bodies were found, but the furniture was literally smashed into fragments, showing that a fearful fight had taken place there. The furniture in the dining room was also demolished.

"Adjoining the dining room was the apartment occupied by Mrs. McGlincy. There she was found literally slashed to pieces with a hatchet. Blood was everywhere, and, as in the room of Wells, there were evidences of a terrible struggle having taken place between the poor woman and her fiendish son-in-law. The other victims were found in other apartments."

The last seen of Dunham he was riding rapidly toward San Jose on a buckskin horse with a heavy Mexican saddle. Family troubles are said to have caused the murder.

The only being in the house to escape alive was a baby one month old, the child of Mrs. Dunham and the alleged murderer.

Colonel McGlincy was one of the California Commissioners to the World's Fair at Chicago.

The only witnesses to the murder were Schaible, who viewed the killing of McGlincy from the barn, and a young neighbor named Ross who saw from behind the barn.

The Colonel, his son and Briscoe were in town last night and did not return until late. Dunham's wife and the baby and Mrs. McGlincy were home. The mania to destroy must have seized Dunham early in the evening from the fact that the bodies of the women were cold when found.

It is surmised that they must have been killed an hour or two before the return of the men. Dunham employed various methods of killing. His wife, with whom he had apparently lived happily, was strangled and clothes were found crowded down her throat.

Minnie Shesler's skull was split open with an ax, and her clothes stuffed in her throat.

Dunham's most brutal work was on Mrs. McGlincy, her head being terribly crushed with an ax.

James K. Wells, Mrs. McGlincy's son, was the first to enter the house on the return of the men and must have met Dunham in the dining room as there are evidences of an awful struggle, the floor being strewn with broken crockery.

He was shot several times. McGlincy, on hearing the disturbance entered but on realizing the seriousness of the situation, fled terror-stricken, screaming murder with all his might, and crying out for help, followed by Dunham.

McGlincy took refuge in the cabin occupied by the hired men. Dunham fired through the door and demanded McGlincy to come out, who, realizing how perilous his situation was, came out and was shot down by Dunham.

Briscoe, who was in the cabin with McGlincy, tried to escape by jumping out of the rear window, but was brought to the ground by a shot through the right lung, killing him instantly. Yet the hired man, Schaible, hid in the hay loft and escaped.

After completing his bloody work, Dunham took a horse from the barn and rode away, but is supposed to be in hiding near the scene.

Although no motive is assigned, Dunham's work seems to have been premeditated, as he destroyed all of his photos, and took a large portrait from the wall with him.

Campbell citizens are greatly excited. Business is at a standstill. They have organized a posse and declare they will lynch Dunham to the nearest tree as soon as he is caught, and he is almost sure to be caught before night.

Newspaper: *San Jose Mercury*
Date: May 28, 1896

The scene at the McGlincy place yesterday was appalling in the extreme. Daybreak revealed features of the butchery that the shadows of night had concealed, and caused even the strongest to shudder and grow faint. Six ghastly forms which had been living beings but a few hours before bore mute evidence to the murderous lust of James C. Dunham.

The officers were busy all day, scouring the surrounding country, but up to an early hour this morning had met with no success. Governor Budd has taken an official cognizance of the enormity of the crime and has offered a reward of $1000 for the arrest and conviction of Dunham. The following notice, accompanied by a picture of the murderer, is being sent over the county and state by Sheriff Lyndon:

> Wanted for murder – James C. Dunham killed Colonel R. P. McGlincy and wife and four other persons about 12:00 last night, May 26, at Campbell, near this city, and escaped on a small buckskin horse, which he will probably soon abandon. He is an expert bicyclist, and may be on a wheel. About thirty-two years of age, nearly 6 feet high, weight 160 to 170 pounds, dark hair and mustache, blue eyes, medium complexion; when last seen he wore black suit, cutaway coat, black soft hat, number nine shoes, and sharp pointed toes. Walks very erect; chin recedes when he laughs. Wire all information to me at my expense. J. H. Lyndon, Sheriff.

Coroner Secord reached the scene of the sextuple murder at an early hour, and the bodies of Colonel R. P. McGlincy and Robert Briscoe, the hired man, were removed from out in the open, where they had fallen and died, to the front room of the residence, and placed upon the floor besides the bullet-riddled corpse of James Wells. The body of Mrs. McGlincy, which lay in the downstairs bedroom, and those of Mrs. Dunham and Minnie Shesler, the servant girl, lying in the sleeping room of the former on the upper floor were not disturbed until after they had been viewed by the coroner's jury.

The puzzling part of the crime was the apparent absence of motive, but that the murderer fancied he had been greatly wronged is very evident. It was established beyond a reasonable doubt that the slaughter was premeditated. As Dunham made away with all of the McGlincy family, save an infant three weeks old—his own son—no one remains to relate to the dread details of the terrible affair from the beginning. This part of the crime committed within doors had to be judged by the appearance of the victims and the appearance of the several rooms. The latter part of the tragedy had eye-witnesses and the connected story is as follows:

James Dunham reached the McGlincy home about 10 o'clock Tuesday night. He had not been home the previous evening, as it was not known when he would return there was no one awaiting him. His wife, the servant girl and Mrs. McGlincy had all retired. Colonel McGlincy and James Wells, his stepson, had gone to an American Protective Association meeting at Campbell. Dunham went upstairs and aroused his wife. What words passed between them no one knows, and the mystery is deepened by a note found on the bureau after the deed had been committed. The note read:

Please say goodbye for me to my dear mother, brother and stepfather. Hattie.

The writing is remarkably like that of Mrs. Dunham, and the note may be genuine, although some are inclined to the belief that Dunham wrote it merely to throw an obstacle in the way of those who might attempt to unravel the intricacies of the murderous web which he was just beginning to weave.

Dunham had secured the ax before he went to his wife's room, but he did not use it upon her. Instead he gagged her, then grasped her by the throat and dislocated her neck by a sudden wrench to one side. No attempt was made to harm the sleeping babe, and, as Dunham was always noted for his brute cunning rather than manly intelligence, it is thought this was done in order that the baby might become the owner of the McGlincy estate after he had exterminated the family.

Minnie Shesler, the servant girl, slept in a room adjoining that of Mrs. Dunham. She had apparently been aroused by the commotion, and, thinking that her mistress might need her aid, she got up from her bed, slipped on a wrapper, buttoned one button and hastened to Mrs. Dunham's room. The murderer stood ready with his ax, and probably before the girl had time to realize that she stood face to face with death the weapon descended, the blow crushing her skull. As she was falling, or as she lay on the floor, Dunham hacked at her four times before he felt satisfied that she was dead.

Dunham was now thoroughly aroused. He was no longer a man, but a fiend. He descended the stairs, the bloody ax in his hand, and entered the room of Mrs. McGlincy, his mother-in-law. Mrs. McGlincy had become alarmed at the commotion upstairs, and she had arisen from her bed and stood near the door of her room. One blow of the ax crushed her skull in a terrible manner, but this was not deemed sufficient, and four more blows were struck before Dunham desisted and left her like he had the servant girl, weltering in blood.

Dunham knew that the men would not be home for nearly an hour, and he busied himself preparing for their reception and for his subsequent flight. He went through all his effects, taking a number of papers, all the cartridges he could find and two revolvers, one of 38 caliber and the other a ferocious-looking 45. His cunning again asserted itself and he went through all of the photograph albums in the house, taking all likenesses of himself and thrusting them in his pocket. A large picture of himself, which was hanging in the reception, or front room, was removed from its frame and disposed of in some manner yet unknown. Only one picture, a small tin-type, escaped him, and that likeness of the murderer is at present in the hands of Sheriff Lyndon.

Having made all arrangements which he thought necessary, Dunham put out all the lights and deliberately sat down in the dark to await the return of the men whom he intended to slaughter in cold blood. He still had the ax, and his stock of weapons now included two revolvers. The thoughts of the man who, with hands red with others' blood, sat in lonely vigil in a house of the dead awaiting other defenseless victims can neither be imagined nor described.

Shortly after 11 o'clock the sound of wheels announced the return of three men, two of whom were returning but to meet a terrible death. Colonel McGlincy and his stepson, James Wells, after turning over the horse in rig to the care of George Schaible, the hired man who accompanied them to the Campbell meeting, went to the house. Dunham was waiting just inside the dining room door. James Wells walked in first, closely followed by Colonel McGlincy. The murderer had his ax raised, but allowed Wells to pass. The weapon was then brought down on Colonel McGlincy, striking him at the outer edge of the right eye, making an ugly cut. As McGlincy fell he screamed, and Wells, turning around, grappled with the fiend, who was intoxicated with the lust of blood. Wells had but recently been severely injured in a bicycle accident and he was still weak, but he made a desperate struggle. The two men swayed to and fro, Wells being forced back into the reception room. Dunham vainly endeavored to use the ax. Twice he struck the wall, as is shown by the dents in the plaster and by particles of plaster clinging to the ax when it was found. He then dropped the weapon and got hold of his revolvers, both of which were used on Wells, who received three 38 and two 45-caliber bullets. Wells was at last shot to death, and sank to the floor, his feet almost touching the fireplace as he stiffened out. The pistols had been held close to his body and the powder set his coat on fire.

While the struggle was going on Colonel McGlincy staggered to his feet, and going into the kitchen climbed out of a window to the side of the house. This progress was shown by a trail of blood and there were crimson fingerprints on the window sill. The wounded man ran toward the cabin where the hired men sleep shouting for help. He was two hundred feet from the house when Dunham, who had just finished Wells, came out the front door and started in pursuit of McGlincy, who, however, ran into the cabin. George Schaible, the young German hired man, who luckily escaped death, was standing at the northwest corner of the barn when he saw Dunham pursuing Colonel McGlincy. The murderer passed without observing him and Schaible quickly entered the barn through a rear window and climbed to the loft. He peered out through a door in the loft and saw Dunham go up on the porch of the cabin. McGlincy was holding the door and the murderer shot several times through the boards. He then shouted: "Come out, Mac, come out! I've got to have you."

"Don't shoot me anymore, Jim," pleaded McGlincy. "I've got two bullets in my body now."

"Come out of that, Mac," was the only response.

"Put up your pistol, Jim, and I'll come out," said the wounded man.

"All right, Mac, I'll do that," replied Dunham, but there was a mockery in his tones, and Colonel McGlincy refused to voluntarily put himself at the mercy of a man whom he knew would shoot him down like a dog.

Dunham then reloaded his pistol and sent a few more shots through the door. He pressed the door open a little, and putting the muzzle of the weapon in his in the opening, fired again. McGlincy was terribly wounded by this time, but he grasped a chair and opened the door. A bullet struck the upraised chair and then Dunham stepped back from the porch and shot McGlincy again, the bullet reaching the heart: McGlincy walked about thirty feet toward the barn and fell dead.

Robert Briscoe was one of the hired men who slept in the cabin. Briscoe had retired, but got up when he heard the shooting. Before he had time to leave the cabin McGlincy rushed in and closed the door. The fusillade of shots followed, some of the bullets passing through the partition which divided the cabin into two rooms. When McGlincy grasped the chair and opened the door Briscoe attempted to break through a rear window.

Dunham, after seeing McGlincy fall, turned to the cabin and shouted: "Come out, Bob." Just then he heard the noise Briscoe made as he jumped through the window. He divined the cause in an instant and rushed to the back of the cabin. He headed Briscoe off and put two bullets into him before he had gone 100 feet. One of the shots struck Briscoe in is heart, and he dropped in his tracks.

The lust for killing did not die out even then. Dunham came back to the front of the cabin and shouted: "George! George! Where are you? Come out here." He was calling for the hired man, who was in the loft holding his breath in abject terror. Receiving no response, Dunham went in the cabin, and lighting a match searched for another victim. When he came out he went into the barn, and bringing out a little buckskin mare, vaulted onto her back. He had taken time to bridle her, but evidently had not looked for a saddle.

As he passed by the house, he probably threw the 45 caliber revolver on the porch, which was found by the neighbors when they entered the house.

The inquest on the bodies of Dunham victims was called a 10:30 A.M., but after a session of three hours an adjournment was taken until 10:00 this morning. The residence was placed in charge of Deputy Constable R. K. Thomas of Campbell and L. C. Ross, with the instruction that admittance was to be refused to the morbid and curious, great numbers of which visited the McGlincy residence yesterday.

Charles Dunham, brother of the murderer, demanded admission and was refused. He said he wanted to see Mrs. Dunham and added that he was engaged to her before his brother married her. After hanging around the house for a few hours, Charles Dunham gave up hope of being admitted to the house and drove back to San Jose, where he resides.

Autopsies were performed on each body by Dr. C. N. Cooper of Campbell and Dr. R. P. Gober of Los Gatos. The bodies were prepared for burial by J. E. McCormick and Edward Arnold, assistants of W. L. Woodrow. The autopsies were very thorough and made Dunham's cold-blooded ferocity appear, if possible, still more appalling.

It was found that Colonel McGlincy had been wounded five times. There was an ax wound just at the outer edge of the right eye, one bullet had gone through his heart, another through his right lung, a third through his right shoulder and a fourth through his right arm.

Mrs. A. M. McGlincy's skull was crushed and shattered in a terrible manner. She had been struck five blows on the head, one blow with the sharp edge of the ax and the other four with the blunt side or back of the weapon.

The cause of Mrs. Hattie B. Dunham's death was a lateral dislocation of the neck, caused by twisting her head violently to one side.

Minnie Shesler's skull was crushed with the bloody end of the ax, and there were five cuts made with the edge, all of which extended to the brain.

James Wells was wounded five times. One bullet entered his chest, passed through the left lung and, coming out of the back, embedded itself in the floor of the room in which he was killed. Another bullet entered from the back, passed through the spine and lower lobe of the left lung and lodged under the skin. One ball entered the left shoulder and another struck the thumb of the left-hand. A ghastly wound was made by a bullet which entered the left jaw and passed out of the cavity of the skull just back of the right ear, then followed the line of the scalp to the center of the head. Either of the shots through the lungs or the one in the jaw was sufficient to cause death.

Robert Briscoe was shot twice. One bullet went through his heart and the other through his right lung.

The McGlincy residence was known as a model country home. The place was furnished in fine style. There was an upright piano in the parlor, and a large number of books by standard authors showed that the family was of the higher order of intelligence. This quiet country home was converted in a night to a veritable charnel house. Those who went through the house yesterday morning met blood and corpses at almost every turn.

Neighbors and strangers stood around in front of the residence and talked of the tragedy, and all expressed the hope that Dunham would be soon caught and lynched. Late in the afternoon a number of lady friends of the McGlincy family were allowed to view the dead, and the eyes of all were filled with tears as they came away.

The body of Minnie Shesler was removed to the residence of her father, Dr. J. A. Shesler, on Marliere Street, near Home. The funeral of the other five victims will take place from the McGlincy residence tomorrow afternoon at 1 o'clock. The internment of Colonel and Mrs. McGlincy will be under the auspices of the Odd Fellows.

James Dunham, the murderer, married into the McGlincy family about a year ago, his bride being Miss Hattie Wells, a daughter of Mrs. McGlincy by her first husband. He has never been considered very bright, old schoolmates stating that he was extremely dull mentally. He had a cheery fashion of greeting people, but there was something about him that prevented many from cultivating his acquaintance. Dunham was lazy and careless in his dress. Of late he had acquired a reputation for closeness in money matters. George Schaible, the surviving hired man, when asked yesterday if Dunham drank, replied that Jim was too stingy to pay anything for liquor. Dunham's marriage is alleged to have been an unhappy one, and that his wife was preparing to apply to the courts for relief. It is also said that on account of a card game at the McGlincy place about six weeks ago the Colonel and Jim had ceased speaking to each other. Dunham has been attending Santa Clara College several months. He rode to and from school on his bicycle, and sometimes went to San Jose and remained overnight. He started out Monday morning, but he did not go back to the orchard home until he went there with murder in his heart. The bicycle cannot now be found by the officers, and they believe Dunham had it secreted not far away. Charles D. Dunham, the brother of the murderer, is employed as a bookkeeper in the city by H. L. Miller, proprietor of the paper house at No. 31 South Second Street. On learning of the tragedy he called upon the officers and offered to do all in his power to assist them in capturing his brother, who he firmly believes has become a maniac.

"There is no doubt," said Charles Dunham, "but that my brother was insane. He was a hard and assiduous worker all his life. He was a graduate of the San Jose High School and recently had been taking a course of Latin and Greek at the Santa Clara College, and he had taxed his brain severely in the effort to accomplish in six weeks what the course prescribed requires six months of study.

"There is not the slightest truth in any report that there was trouble in the family. My brother and his wife were married a little over a year ago. He loved his wife dearly and she reciprocated his love deeply. The whole family loved him and even idolized him, and when I was out to the house a week ago to visit them I found them enjoying perfect happiness. James' wife then told me that they all were so happy and that James adored the little one just born to them on the 4th of May. At morning and night she said that James played with the child as if his entire life was wrapped up in it.

"Yes, I want to see the James is incarcerated as soon as possible and I want to give the officers as much assistance as is in my power to locate him. I have no idea where he might have gone, for I know of no place where he could secure protection and shelter, or where he might apply for assistance. He is 31 years old and I am 25. My sister, who attends the Normal School, is about 22 years of age. This will surely kill her, or it will be a severe blow to her at least, for she is not strong, and since the death of our mother, three years ago, she has been almost broken-hearted, for they loved each other so dearly."

Mrs. Hattie B. Dunham, wife of the murderer and who met death of his hands, was 26 years of age, and a graduate of the State Normal School. She was considered highly educated and refined and many expressed surprise when she married Dunham.

Tom Lovelady states that he was at the Black place, a short distance from McGlincy's on Tuesday evening about 9:30 o'clock. Two men passed by on bicycles. He recognized one of them as Dunham, not only by his features, which showed plainly in the bright moonlight, but by his voice, as he was talking as he went by with his companion. Who this companion was has not been discovered. Dunham possibly got someone to go with him on some pretext or other, as it is not likely that he told his real intentions.

At 1:30 o'clock this morning Detective Robert Anderson and District Attorney Parrington left town armed with double-barrel shotguns. They had received a letter from a resident near Guadalupe that a man answering the description of Dunham was seen passing his place early in the evening. The letter was given to a streetcar conductor and then to one of the officers. They will not return until tonight.

Newspaper: *San Jose Mercury*
Date: May 28, 1896

Coroner Secord was notified of the murder at 3:15 o'clock in the morning. He left an hour later, accompanied by his official stenographer, Mrs. M. V. Collins.

J. A. Shesler, the father of Minnie Shesler, the murdered servant girl, was the first witness examined. He testified as to the girl being 28 years of age and a native of Fostoria, Ohio. That she came to this county in 1881 and had been in the employ of Colonel McGlincy for about two months. He had heard his daughter say that there was trouble existing in the McGlincy family and that she had heard Colonel McGlincy say that Dunham was "kinder trifling." He understood from what his daughter had said that a lawsuit was likely to arise between Dunham and Colonel McGlincy in regard to injuries which Dunham was alleged to have sustained while working upon the place. He could advance no cause for the murder of his daughter.

Edward W. Parr was called and testified to Colonel McGlincy's domestic relations. He had considered it a very peaceful home, and knew that the tie between Colonel McGlincy and his wife was a very affectionate one.

Charles Sterret, who met Dunham on the road, was the next witness examined. He stated that he left Campbell about twenty minutes to 12 o'clock and started for his home on the Coke Ranch by way of Campbell Avenue. After walking for about ten minutes he heard someone say that there was trouble at McGlincy's. In a few moments he heard the footsteps of a horse on the San Jose Road and hurried to the corner, as he thought that it was someone hurrying to town for assistance who could tell him what was the matter. He hollowed out: "Who are you?"

Dunham slacked up and whirled around, saying: "Did you see George?" Witness said no. "Dunham," continued the witness, "asked 'Did you see a man on horseback?' I replied 'Yes.' He asked, 'What color was his horse?'

"I replied bay, and asked him who he was.

"He said, 'Who are you?' By that time he pulled his hand up from his side, as if he had a pistol, and asked, 'What is your name?'

"'Who are you?' I asked in reply: but then I told him I was stopping at the Coke Ranch, and asked, 'What is the matter at McGlincy's?'

"He replied, 'Who is McGlincy?'

"I replied that I had heard a fellow on horseback say there was trouble over there. He asked 'Who told you?' I replied that I had heard a man say as he went by that there was trouble at McGlincy's."

The witness stated that he went direct to McGlincy's house after leaving Dunham. He was satisfied Dunham did not know him. He was positive the man he met was Dunham. He understood Dunham to be referring to George Schaible when he said "George." Dunham, he said, went on the Infirmary Road to Campbell Avenue and then turned and went south.

Newspaper: *San Jose Mercury*
Date: May 28, 1896

From the time the murder was announced yesterday morning in San Jose the sheriff and deputies were all exerting every effort toward the capture of the murderer.

Sheriff Lyndon and Undersheriff Benson, at 7 o'clock yesterday morning, went to the McGlincy home for the second time and made a thorough search of the house and its surroundings. The officers ferreted into every nook and corner, for anything that might serve as evidence as to the motive for the crime or for information that might serve the officers in their search for the criminal. Many letters and cards were found, but nothing of an unusual character. From the letters is it was gleaned that Dunham had been in business in various parts of the state. At Chico-Butte County, he had conducted a nursery under the name of Butte County Nursery.

At one time he conducted a bicycle agency on El Dorado Street, Stockton. He was also in business in Sacramento and San Diego.

After the search of the house, Sheriff Lyndon, with Deputy Reynolds of Los Gatos, took in all the roads in the vicinity of Los Gatos, Almaden and intervening country.

Rumors were afloat that a man was seen riding a horse through Los Gatos at a lively rate yesterday morning at 2 o'clock and went up the Santa Cruz grade. This could not be confirmed. Another rumor was to the effect that a man was seen riding a horse at the same hour on the Los Gatos and Almaden road. These rumors and various others were chased down by Sheriff Lyndon, but to no avail.

Telegraphic messages were sent out by the Sheriff early yesterday morning to the officers throughout the county and adjoining counties and responsive message received, so it was certain that outlets were all guarded.

All that is possible for the Sheriff to do in one day has been done and now much will depend upon the efficiency of neighboring officials, who will be doubly incited to active work by the prospect of a larger reward.

Governor James H. Budd telegraphed District Attorney Harrington yesterday afternoon the following message:

> *A reward will be offered in such sum as you may deem proper and within the limit allowed by law. Announce the fact that $500 will be given for the arrest and conviction of James C. Dunham. If that is not sufficient wire me and I will increase the amount. You may notify peace officers this reward will be given.*

In response to this dispatch, District Attorney Harrington suggested to the Governor that the reward be $1000. This amount will be given by the State, and cards will be issued to that effect this morning, and also bearing the word that the Supervisors will probably increase the reward.

Sheriff Lyndon entertains the opinion that Dunham has gone south, and will travel at night and sleep day times. Dunham is thoroughly acquainted with nearly all of the country between here and San Diego, having camped out and traveled through it.

Dr. McGraw reported at the Sheriff's office last evening an incident that caused an investigation. About 6 o'clock a man came to his house on East San Fernando Street. Dr. McGraw's son went to the door and conversed with a stranger. The fellow asked for some woman, the name of whom the boy did not remember. The boy was impressed with the seeming embarrassment of the stranger, and, on returning, mentioned the fact that the man acted queerly. His description of the man tallied with that of Dunham, with the exception that he wore a dark satin shirt. Dunham was accustomed to wear white linen shirts.

Sheriff Lyndon received a dispatch last evening from Sheriff Ballou a San Luis Obispo to the effect that he will be here tonight with his bloodhounds and will engage in the search for Dunham.

At 11:30 o'clock the Sheriff returned from the Los Gatos and Almaden country and was almost exhausted from his day's work. He had heard nothing of any definite character as to the course the murderer took.

Newspaper: *San Jose Mercury*
Date: May 28, 1896

In an interview with a Mercury representative last evening, Vice-President Rev. Robert E. Kenna of Santa Clara College gave the following account of James Dunham's career at that institution:

"He entered the College as a scholar on February 24 last," said Rev. Father Kenna. "He came to me a few days before to make the arrangements and entered regularly upon his duties on that day. When I learned his age, and I knew from his appearance that he was nearing 30, I was surprised when he told me that he wanted a thorough classical education. He realized that it would require four years to get his degree and started in his work with that knowledge. I pointed out the difficulties and rather discouraged the young man, but he was determined to go at the work. My impression is—although I'm not certain that he told me so—that he had an idea after he finished his college education to study for the law.

"In beginning his studies Dunham entered the most advanced grammar class. He had much Latin and Greek to make up, and for that purpose entered a coaching class in those studies. In that way it was intended that he should do a great deal of extra work in a short time. He understood that and applied himself diligently to the task. There is no doubt that in doing this he studied very hard, and perhaps over-taxed his mental strength. His standing in Latin and Greek thus far is 84 and 88, which is very good. In deportment he stood 100. Of course in his other studies—that he did not have to make up so much in—he was also pushing right ahead. In penmanship he stood 72 in March and 80 in April, showing that he was improving. Dunham's studies were grammar, arithmetic, history, geography, elocution, Latin, Greek, reading, spelling and penmanship. I have recently finished his report of standing for March and April and was intending to hand it to him the first time I had an opportunity.

"In many of his classes Dunham was associated with boys many of whom were not half his age. This is one of the embarrassments and difficulties that I told him when he first entered the college that he would labor under. He did not think that this would give him any trouble, however, and I never heard any of the boys making any sport of him. This was probably due to his very quiet disposition and manner. He was in a degree inapproachable. He was always very polite and would bow to those with whom he was acquainted, but he very seldom showed a disposition to talk to anyone, and he seemed to be a very hard person to become very well acquainted with. He was, I might say, a silent man. He rarely if ever smiled, and had what might be called a far-away expression. Of course these things did not excite in my mind any suspicions of insanity or of any desperate tendency that he might have had. I only recall these peculiarities in light of the terrible thing that has happened. But for this awful tragedy the man's acts would never have been deemed worthy of a special remark.

"There is a rumor among the students here today that cannot be traced to the authentic source that Dunham had a pistol in his possession one day when he was at school about a month ago. This was not reported at the time to any of his preceptors or it would have been investigated and some action taken in regard to it in case the report had proved true.

"One noon hour I noticed that Dunham did not have any lunch and I invited him to lunch. He declined, saying that he ate only two meals a day. I have now learned the rather strange fact that sometimes he brought a lunch and then did not eat it. At first he spent his recesses in hard study, but recently he seemed to realize that this was telling on him. He did not say so, as far as I know, but from his actions it would seem that he made up his mind to take some recreation during lunch time. He did not wish to play with boys on the College grounds, so he secured a rubber pulling machine, such as are much used for exercising the arms and chest muscles. I allowed him to use a room in which he could go through these exercises with the machine, and he pursued them diligently, I believe.

"I did not ask him that question, and I did not know when Dunham entered the College that he was a married man. We learned this fact when we saw the notice in a paper of the birth of his child. Then some of the boys asked him about it, and he acknowledged that he was the James Dunham referred to in the birth notice.

"He told me on entering that he was not a Catholic, but we were never aware that he had any very pronounced anti-Catholic views. There are always more or less Protestant students in the College. Once, when I told him that he was not required, being a Protestant, to attend some religious services, he said he would go with the rest of the students anyhow. He attended some lectures and a three-day retreat, when studies were suspended.

"Besides being quiet and polite Dunham seemed to be considerate of others. In going back and forth from his home to the College he rode a bicycle. He was always particular to keep a warning bell in good order on his machine. I think he was about the only bicycle rider around the institution who was particular in that regard.

"The last time Dunham was at the College was on Wednesday, the morning before the killing. So far as can be learned he did not act different than from what he had on other occasions. He always took his books home every night, and Wednesday morning at the usual study hour he appeared with them. He was seldom late to school, and when he was he always politely stated his excuse to the preceptor. On Wednesday there were examinations in which Dunham had no part, and in the afternoon there were to be no studies, so he was free to go soon after he arrived at the school. What is peculiar is that for the first time, so far as can be learned, he left his books on his desk instead of taking them home. He unwrapped them from the package in which he usually carried them on the road. When he left he did not wrap the books up again, but pushed them aside loosely. This may or may not be a significant fact in the case. He was due to resume his studies this morning, and in view of the fact that he might be insane we were somewhat alarmed by the bare possibility that he might come around and run amok among the students. At our suggestion Marshall Lovell was on hand to watch, but, of course, Dunham did not appear."

Newspaper: *San Francisco Chronicle*
Date: May 28, 1896

SAN JOSE - District Attorney Bert Herrington has probably known as much about Dunham as anyone here. Speaking of him, Herrington said: "He was always a determined, desperate fellow—a man of violent and ungovernable temper. He used to live near me at Santa Clara, and I know he was a fellow who was up to all kinds of devilment; as a boy he would never stand the blame, but would always put it off on somebody else. There was a rumor years ago that he chased his sister and mother through the yard with a hatchet."

County Assessor Spitzer says Dunham's mother had the most violent temper of any human being he ever knew. He said that she was for years known as "Kate, the Terror." He thinks Dunham probably inherited the peculiarity, which borders close to mania. The murderer's mother died three years ago. Tyler Beach, proprietor of the St. James Hotel, remembers her well as a woman of most arbitrary and ungovernable impulses. While few persons are heard to say they believe Dunham is insane, the opinion in general is that his temper was very violent.

Charles Dunham, the murderer's brother, bears a good reputation here. When he heard of the murders this morning he said to his sister: "Jim has gone insane and killed Hattie." He did not tell his sister that her brother had killed five others.

Charles Dunham went to the police today and offered to be of any assistance he could in securing the arrest of his brother. He says he is insane. In regard to money, Charles told Acting Police Chief Anderson that his brother had about $1000. District Attorney Harrington thinks Dunham had about $1500 in local banks, but he has not yet succeeded in locating it.

Rev. Father Raggio, one of the officers of Santa Clara College, said tonight: "Dunham is not a regular student of the College. He has had some sort of connection as a special student recently. He was studying telegraphy, I believe, and possibly some other branches, but was not a close attendant, even for the short time he has been registered. He was not at the college Monday at all. I know very little about him. He has not been a student in this way long enough to become much acquainted. I cannot tell anything of his disposition. All I know is that he is not a student, and has had only a brief connection with our school."

The police state that Dunham has been preparing for his crime for some days, the last two days before the deed being spent in immediate preparation. Those officials think it probable that he had food and water stored at some secure place, and went there directly afterward.

It is the theory of the two witnesses to the murder that Dunham's motive was largely greed, and that he spared his babe that it might inherit the McGlincy property, estimated to be worth $75,000. Those who have seen the most of Dunham and who know him best say that greed is a large part of his makeup.

Schaible reported last night: "Dunham was always having trouble in the family. He had a row with the servant girl on Monday morning over his breakfast. He left here some time Monday and did not get back until about 8:30 at night."

Those who know most about Dunham say that his wife was very weary of him as a husband, because of his violent temper and arbitrary manner. She was a graduate of the State Normal School and had been a student at the State University, and was a woman of considerable culture. Schaible, however, says that Dunham and his wife were not badly mated in that way, as he always had a book in his hand and was particularly devoted to his religion and to all studies pertaining to it.

Newspaper: *San Francisco Chronicle*
Date: May 28, 1896

The evidence of George Schaible was taken and he swore that he had been working on the ranch since the 23rd of January, and that he had worked there two years ago for seven months. He knew some of the family troubles of Colonel McGlincy and Dunham from what McGlincy told him. "He told me," said the witness, "that Dunham was going to sue him last year for injuries received by falling from a ladder while picking fruit two years ago." Off the witness stand Schaible said the suit was to be for $14,000. The witness said that Dunham claimed to his wife about a month ago that he had been robbed of $1000 but McGlincy never believed the story. Witness said that McGlincy did not speak to Dunham. A cool feeling had existed between the men for several weeks. Schaible played cards with the men nearly every night until two or three weeks ago when the games suddenly ceased and McGlincy and Dunham never spoke thereafter. That was before Dunham had said he had been robbed of $1000.

Newspaper: *Sacramento Bee*
Date: May 28, 1896

James Dunham, who murdered Colonel R. P. McGlincy, Mrs. McGlincy, James K Wells, Minnie Shesler, Robert Briscoe and Mrs. Hattie Dunham, his wife, near San Jose on Tuesday night, was quite well known in Sacramento.

During the last State Fair, Dunham and his wife conducted a restaurant and lemonade stand at the corner of 15th and M streets.

They were supplied by a local house with the necessary crockery and glassware, but they were subsequently dispossessed of those articles by the manager of the concern. A suit for damages followed in which the merchant was mulcted to the amount of $80.00.

Dunham and his wife occupied apartments at 719½ J Street from September, 1895, to an early date in January of this year.

Yesterday Sheriff Johnson and Deputy Hinters made inquiries regarding his residence here, and from their investigations they are convinced that Dunham is too well known to come here without being apprehended by the authorities.

Governor Budd today offered a reward of $1000 for the arrest and conviction of Dunham.

Newspaper: *San Jose Mercury*
Date: May 29, 1896

James Dunham was seen and interviewed last evening, and Sheriff Lyndon confidently expects to have him in custody before 9 o'clock this morning.

The fugitive murderer, bruised and exhausted, is now somewhere in the vicinity of Mount Hamilton and the probability of his escape is so remote as to be almost impossible.

Dunham was seen at 6:30 o'clock last evening near Smiths Creek Hotel. He was hungry and exhausted and the little buckskin horse he rode was tired.

He was endeavoring to reach the San Joaquin Valley, and made inquiries as to the way.

Sheriff Lyndon, accompanied by Sheriff Ballou and his bloodhounds and the posse of determined men, are now on the ground.

It is thought all avenues of escape are closed.

Word was received last evening shortly before 7 o'clock from Smiths Creek that Dunham was seen in that vicinity not more than a half hour before and was making his way up to Mount Hamilton.

In response to the message Sheriff Lyndon hastened back to San Jose and shortly before 8 o'clock was making rapid headway with the posse of efficient officers for Smiths Creek, and with a feeling of confidence that he would not return without Dunham.

The story of Dunham's brief stay in the vicinity of Smiths Creek is anything but the expected.

Riding the same horse upon which he effected his flight from the Campbell District after the awful deed on Tuesday night, bareback and without bridle, his face bruised and scratched in the terrible fight with those he slayed, his feet wrapped in clothes to conceal the human blood. Dunham was not one who most persons would care to meet in a lonely country, nor one from whom a protracted interview could be expected.

But such he was, and with him Oscar S. Parker and Everett Snell conversed for several minutes last evening at 6:30 o'clock on a trail about half a mile from Smiths Creek and a like distance from the Mount Hamilton Road.

Parker resides in the cabin on the Bob Morrow Ranch, a half mile from the Smiths Creek Hotel, and Snell stays at the hotel. They had been in the direction of the hotel, and were returning toward the cabin when they spied Dunham on the trail. His horse was moving slowly, and was evidently almost worn out.

Dunham seemed not in the least inclined to avoid them, and when they came nearer a conversation was begun in a commonplace way.

From the usual salutations they drifted into subjects which soon convinced Parker and Snell that they were talking to the man most wanted of all.

The color of the horse, the fact that the rider was in the mountains without either bridle or saddle and everything else about the man and horse indicated who he was. To Snell there was no doubt, for he had known Dunham in the valley.

Parker says Dunham put a whole lot of socks on over his shoes. This precaution he had doubtless taken to either cover up his blood-stained shoes or he had discarded his shoes and employed the socks for warmth.

His face had been severely beaten and scratched. These injuries he had no doubt received in the struggle with Wells.

As he rode he carried a sack in which he said he had provisions.

Throughout his talk with Parker and Snell, he evinced considerable anxiety to get across the mountains.

His conversation was mainly with Parker.

Dunham gave Snell and Parker at once the impression that he was dazed, for they first accosted him by saying: "Hello, where did you come from, the San Joaquin?"

To this Dunham hesitated and then responded, "Yes."

"I've been up to the cabin there," he said, "and broke in. I haven't had anything to eat for two days, and had to get something, so I got in, and I took some bacon and prunes."

Parker said: "That's all right," and invited him to stay all night.

"No," replied Dunham, "I must push on," but it was only after some hesitation that he refused.

He made a move as if to put his horse in the stable, but seemed to suddenly change his mind.

He then asked: "How far it is it to Smiths Creek? I guess I'll go up Smiths Creek to go over to the San Joaquin."

Parker was anxious for him not to go that way as it would be harder for the officials to get at him, so he replied: "It will be better for you not to go that way, for there are some officers over in that country looking for cattle thieves and they may run on to you."

Dunham said: "Well, I don't want any of that."

"Yes," replied Parker, "they might catch you and hold you for a cattle thief."

Dunham said, "That is so. But how can I get out of here?"

"Take the trail for the Mount Hamilton Road," was Parker's advice, his idea being that Dunham could be caught easier in that direction.

"Which way you traveling?" asked Parker.

"I've got to get into the San Joaquin Valley. Can you tell me whether I can go over by trail," was Dunham's reply.

"You will have to take the Mount Hamilton Road," said Parker.

Dunham said he had made a search through the cabin for ammunition, but failed to find any.

"Say, can't I get to Mount Hamilton by a trail?" he asked, evidently hoping that he might avoid that much of the road.

"No, sir," said Parker; "your only way to Mount Hamilton is by the main road."

Dunham remarked again that he was very tired, and Parker extended him another invitation to spend the night there, but he would not consent, yet it is thought that he would have accepted the invitation had Snell been out of the way, for it could be discerned that he was afraid of Snell, whom he recognized.

Snell started along the trail toward the hotel to notify the Sheriff by telephone. As soon as Snell was out of hearing Dunham asked, "Who is that?"

Parker replied: "Everett Snell."

Dunham immediately answered, "I'll have to push on to the San Joaquin," and then said goodbye and parted.

Dunham's sole purpose seemed to be to reach the San Joaquin Valley.

Snell started ahead of Parker for Smiths Creek to notify the officers, and Parker soon followed on the same mission.

They say that if they had known the thoughts of each other they would have kept watch of him, but when they got together, Dunham was gone.

He went out of sight behind a knoll in the trail, and was going toward the road.

All this information was given the Sheriff upon his arrival at Smiths Creek, and as soon as possible an outline of action was decided upon.

It was concluded that the most effective method would be to start out in different directions and make a thorough search of fences and trails.

They found themselves handicapped by not having a sufficient number of saddle horses, only five being on hand.

These were put into service at once, two parties being formed.

Newspaper: *San Jose Mercury*
Date: May 29, 1896

The evening train which arrives here at 5 o'clock from San Luis Obispo brought Sheriff Ballou of that place with his two bloodhounds. The announcement that the hounds were to arrive caused a large crowd of people to assemble at the depot, and when Sheriff Lyndon and Sheriff Ballou drove into the jail yard there was a crowd of people on hand to view the visitors.

The two hounds are rather small in stature and are known as Trim and Flora. They are closely built and extremely nervous, swerving against their collars continually as though anxious to get away. Their constant sniffing suggested their acute sense of smell, and caused many to remark that if they once got the trail, Dunham would have a serious task to perform if he escapes them.

"If there is a trail above ground these dogs will follow it to the end," said Sheriff Ballou, who pulled at their chains as he stood with a dog whip hung over his shoulder. "Of course, they may not be of service in this case, for the ground in the neighborhood of the murder has been trampled over by hundreds, I understand. The dogs will get various scents, and if we can once get them on the right one, they will be of service."

Newspaper: *San Jose Mercury*
Date: May 29, 1896

R. H. Hammonds and J. E. Wing, who reside near Campbell, stated to a Mercury reporter yesterday that they rode from Campbell to McGlincy's place Tuesday evening about 9 o'clock to get cherries, by order of James Wells, and they suppose Thomas E. Lovelady mistook them for Dunham and a companion. They were in the orchard for about thirty-five minutes. The house was dark while they were there and they heard no noise. They had left Wells at Campbell to attend the American Protective Association meeting.

Newspaper: *San Jose Mercury*
Date: May 29, 1896

The funeral of Miss Minnie Shesler, daughter of Dr. and Mrs. W Shesler, one of the victims of murderer Dunham, took place yesterday afternoon at 1:30 o'clock from the First Christian Church. All seats in the church were filled with sorrowing friends who had known the young woman, and the members of the Christian Endeavor Society of the church were present in a body to pay their respects to their deceased member. Miss Shesler was also a member of Kate B. Sherwood Camp, Daughters of Veterans, and this organization was also present. There were many beautiful floral tributes.

The sermon was delivered by Rev. B. B. Burton, pastor of the church. He delivered a touching address, speaking of Miss Shesler's good qualities as a Christian and as a dutiful child of a bereaved family.

A quartet rendered the hymns "Safe in the Arms of Jesus," "Rock of Ages," and "Nearer My God to Thee."

At the grave, after prayer by Rev. Mr. Burton, the Daughters of Veterans conducted the service according to their ritual.

The funeral of Colonel R. P. McGlincy, his wife, James K. Wells, Mrs. Dunham and James Briscoe will be held from the late residence of the deceased this afternoon at 1 o'clock. The interment of Colonel and Mrs. McGlincy and Briscoe will be under the auspices of the Odd Fellows. They will be buried in the family plot in Oak Hill Cemetery.

Newspaper: *San Francisco Chronicle*
Date: May 29, 1896

Today we learned of comments by Mrs. H. M. Parker, who acted as a nurse for Mrs. Dunham when her child was born. "I was there thirteen days in all," said Mrs. Parker, "and I learned considerable about Dunham's home life."

According to Mrs. Parker's story, Dunham showed his wife no more respect than if she had been a beast. He neglected all her requests, no matter how simple. If she wanted so trivial a thing as a glass of water or a fan he would say, "Let your father get that for you."

One day Mrs. Dunham said to her nurse: "What kind of a man do you think I have for a husband, when he tells me he will take my baby to Mexico, start a gambling-house and saloon there, and bring up my child a Catholic?" This is almost the only evidence in any way bearing on Dunham's religious prejudices.

Mrs. Parker testified that she learned while in the house that Mrs. McGlincy had much ill feeling toward her son-in-law. She told Mrs. Parker that Dunham abused his wife and he stole her watch. "Mrs. Dunham herself told me," said Mrs. Parker, "that somebody stole her jewelry and silverware. She did not say it was her husband, though Mrs. McGlincy thought so. The only thing that Dunham seemed to be in the least attached to was the babe. He held it in his arms a great deal and used to lie on the bed with it, proud of it."

Mrs. Parker describes how Dunham neglected to buy his wife mosquito netting, though requested day after day to do so. He made no apologies for his neglect, but stolidly refused to do anything for the comfort of his wife.

From the conversations of the women of the household, Mrs. Parker learned that Dunham once or twice humiliated his wife saying: "Your father was a sheep thief." She retaliated by saying: "You stole my watch." There were many evidences that there was much discord in the house.

Mrs. Parker's description of Dunham's conduct when his wife asked him to buy needful articles give a good idea of his stubborn character. "I asked him to get some netting," said she, "but he made no reply. When I asked again it was the same thing—not the least answer. To other requests for needful things he would say: 'let Mac get it' or 'let Jimmie buy it,' always refusing to turn a hand himself."

Mrs. Parker stated that Dunham never ate with the family. The hired men and McGlincy ate early, then the ladies ate their breakfast, after which Dunham would crawl out of bed and eat just before going to school. He seemed sullen and morose rather than violent or cross.

The nurse was told by Mrs. McGlincy to present her bill to Dunham at once, as he had just foreclosed a mortgage on a house in The Willows. "Mrs. McGlincy told me," said Mrs. Parker, "that if Dunham did not pay the bill to present it to McGlincy, and if he refused, to present it to her. I have never presented it to anybody, so I do not know whether he would have paid it or not."

Newspaper: *San Francisco Chronicle*
Date: May 29, 1896

George T. Brewer of 729 Turk Street, brother-in-law of the murdered Mrs. McGlincy, believes that spite and a desire for gain were the motives which prompted James Dunham to slaughter the whole family of his father-in-law. Mr. Brewer has spent the past two days at the scene of the murders, where he has been in charge so far as he did not interfere with the duties of the officers. Last evening he was in his own home, which is guarded by armed men, for Mr. Brewer fears the cool-headed villain.

"During the two days I have spent at the scene of that horrid butchery," said Mr. Brewer last evening, "I have had ample time to reason out the motive of the murderer. I have never met him but twice, and would scarcely know him now were I to stumble upon him on the street, but my recollection of our first meeting is so vivid that I have never thought of the man without a shudder. He was repulsive to me.

"There is no question in my mind that he murdered Colonel McGlincy and his whole family because he knew that the valuable estate would then revert to him through his son, and he betook pleasure in his bloody work because he had a personal spite to revenge.

"Of his inability to get along with Colonel McGlincy and Mr. Wells has already been said, and it is all true. He was mean and avaricious in his dealings with the family. He is a natural crank in his habits, requiring that his food be prepared in a certain way.

"My theory is that he never intended to murder the hired men— only the people in the house. And he intended to do it all with the keen-bladed ax with which he murdered Mrs. McGlincy and leave no clew, but his plans miscarried. He knew the habits of everyone in the household and knew that McGlincy and Wells had gone to San Jose and knew when they would return. He knew, too, that it was customary for young Wells to assist in putting up the horse, and that the old man would most likely enter the house first. No doubt he counted upon the fact that Wells had not yet recovered from a bicycle accident which came near ending his life. He would be too weak to offer much resistance.

"Dunham spent the night previous to the murders in San Jose. He did not ride out to the McGlincy house until 9:30 at night. It was his intention to murder all the women noiselessly, and he did it. Mrs. McGlincy made an awful struggle for life, but had not the strength to cry out.

"Then the murderer sat down, almost in the blood of his victims, to await the homecoming of the men. He probably intended to fell the old man as he entered the door with the ax. Wells was to have met the same fate. Then the fiend would have ridden swiftly and silently back to town on his wheel, ready to prove an alibi in case suspicion should fall upon him and be ready to dissemble over the lifeless body of his wife.

"But his plan failed because he had not counted upon the strength and vitality of McGlincy. The old man was undoubtedly struck down at the door but revived while the murderer was engaged with Wells, and escaped through the window to the shanty. Dunham was compelled to use his pistol to save his own miserable life, and it was through its use that his villainy was discovered.

"Don't talk to me of his insanity. He was as sane as you or I, but a natural-born villain and murderer. He did not act like an insane man. There was method in his madness from start to finish. He wanted the property. By killing off the whole family he could secure it. He planned cleverly and executed well up to a certain point, when the merest chance, you might say, undid him. He cared not a snap of your fingers for human life. Affection for wife or babe was to him a thing unknown. He has gained the property, but will forfeit his life for it if justice is meted out to him.

Newspaper: *San Francisco Chronicle*
Date: May 29, 1896

SACRAMENTO – The police of this city tell an interesting story of James Dunham, the brutal San Jose murderer, who was here with his wife during the last State Fair. Dunham's wife, it seems, one morning missed a watch and some other jewelry. After speaking to her husband about it, she reported the matter to the police who, after a few days' work, traced the articles to a pawn shop and found they had been left there by Dunham. He was confronted with the evidence and confessed the theft in the presence of his wife. Owning to the circumstances no prosecution followed, but the affair seemed to make a decided difference between the two. Those who knew the couple relate stories of extreme brutality on Dunham's part toward his wife.

The couple came to this city last August from Stockton, riding up on bicycles. They stopped at Mrs. E. W. River's residence, near the corner of Twelfth and E Streets, and when the Fair opened Dunham obtained the privilege of conducting a lunch stand at Agricultural Park.

On one occasion, while conducting this stand, Dunham's wife did something he did not like, and he flew into a violent rage and made the most brutal threats against her life if she ever repeated the offense. Mrs. Dunham was frightened at the time, but matters soon quieted down. She was a woman who evidently thought a great deal of her husband, despite his brutality.

Newspaper: *San Jose Mercury*
Date: May 30, 1896

About 10 o'clock yesterday morning Sheriffs Lyndon and Ballou, while going through Indian Gulch, which is situated between Smiths Creek and Mount Hamilton just above Sulphur Creek and about a mile and a half from Smiths Creek, ran across the buckskin horse which Dunham had been riding and which he took from the McGlincy ranch on the night of the murder. The horse was found leisurely grazing. It was running loose but about forty yards away were found evidences of Dunham having camped there on the previous night. The rope which was around the horse's head was found at this place which showed that Dunham had abandoned it for good. The horse displayed no evidence of having been ridden hard. The horse's back was sore but this was evidently the result of injuries received from a rope which had been tied around Dunham's coat, which he used as a substitute for saddle.

Having found the horse Sheriffs Lyndon and Ballou knew that they were in the immediate neighborhood of the murderer and pursued their search with renewed energy. The bloodhounds were let loose and they followed the trail of Dunham to the creek, but here it became apparent that Dunham had thoroughly soaked his feet, which prevented the dogs from further following the trail. Sheriff Lyndon at once organized his posse four abreast and marched up on one side of the canyon and down the other side.

While thus searching, about an hour after the horse was found, the posse heard a gunshot, which seemed to come from the canyon about a mile and a half distant. They went to the vicinity where the shot was fired and made a thorough search to ascertain if Dunham had shot himself. There were no apparent evidences of any man being in the vicinity and no sign of a body was found. The first thought of Sheriff Lyndon was that Dunham had committed suicide, but this was soon dispelled after his thorough search for the body had been made. It is possible, however, that Dunham, dead or alive, is concealed in the brush, as the canyon is steep and rugged and is almost impassable on account of the thick growing brush. About 4 o'clock in the afternoon Sheriff Lyndon left Indian Gulch, taking the horse to Smiths Creek, where it was placed in the stable.

Oscar Parker stated last night: "I am certain that Dunham has plenty of money with him. When he called at my place both of his pockets were bulging out, and I am very certain they were filled with coin. If Dunham could reach clear country he would have sufficient money to facilitate his escape. I think he will endeavor to reach the country about Livermore, knowing that this will enable him to use his money to advantage in the way of buying food and getting passage on trains.

Sheriff Lyndon was nearly exhausted last night. Since 1 o'clock Wednesday morning he has had but three hours of sleep until last evening, and he was forced to take some rest in order to be able to continue the search advantageously. As soon as he received notice of the murder he went to the scene and secured particulars. Since that time he has been with the three hours' intermission stated and been constantly at work in his efforts to capture the murderer.

Newspaper: *San Jose Mercury*
Date: May 30, 1896

The scene in and about Smiths Creek Hotel last night was one of great animation. The hotel is made the rendezvous of the posse upon the hunt for Dunham, and is kept open day and night. With about thirty men heavily armed it has a decidedly warlike appearance. In the corners Winchester rifles are stacked, and bulging from the pockets of the men can be seen the handles of large pistols. The men sit about the room; some in chairs with their feet upon tables and others sit upon the tables and discuss the situation from every point of view. The majority of them indulge in smoking or chewing tobacco while they converse. The scene has been aptly compared to a gathering in a hotel at an old time mining camp. Among the number are many who are thoroughly familiar with the surrounding country and the information they give is valuable to those who are strangers. A spirit of determination to catch Dunham is manifested by all. Sleep is a luxury indulged in by few in the hours of darkness and fog which interrupt the murderer hunt and are passed impatiently.

Manager Snell serves meals at all hours and has shown much courtesy to the Sheriff's attaches and his guests, which is duly appreciated. The Sheriff expressed his gratitude to Manager Snell for his promptness in notifying him of the presence of Dunham in that vicinity.

The fog upon the mountain last night and early this morning was so dense that it was difficult to see but a few feet away. Those upon the watch could only wait for the breaking of the day to enable them to make any further search.

Newspaper: *San Jose Mercury*
Date: May 30, 1896

News regarding the movements of Sheriff Lyndon and posse in their hunt for murderer James Dunham was sought with a feverish and constantly increasing interest by the people of San Jose and vicinity yesterday.

From an early hour in the morning until late in the evening groups of people on the streets were discussing the chase. The number of country people upon the streets was decidedly noticeable, particularly from Campbell and the vicinity surrounding the scene of the murders. After the funeral a number of people came to San Jose from that town, and rumors of a preparation for a lynching were thick. Each new rumor, and there were many, was greedily received and discussed. The people seemed to be expecting sensational news at any moment, and were prepared to give credence to the most improbable rumors. Early in the day a telephone message from Smiths Creek stated that heavy firing had been heard in the neighborhood of the San Ysabel Valley, and though authority for this statement was not given many accepted it as evidence of a fight between Dunham and the officers. This prepared the people for news of a fight and had the effect of increasing the excitement.

There was a report last evening that the number of determined citizens of Campbell, well armed, had posted themselves along the road from Mount Hamilton, and their intention was to take the prisoner from the Sheriff's posse and lynch him in case he should be brought in.

Indian Gulch, the place in which Dunham was supposed to be hiding, is described as being almost impenetrable. It is several miles long and very deep, with almost precipitous sides. The gulch is about half way between Smiths Creek and Mount Hamilton, and about three miles southwest of the main road. On account of the thick brush, it is impossible to proceed along the sides of the gulch, and going up the bottom it is necessary for hunters and others to crawl.

Newspaper: *San Jose Mercury*
Date: May 30, 1896

As the past life of James C. Dunham becomes more plainly outlined it is conclusively shown that the man who murdered six defenseless people last Tuesday night possessed a cruel and vindictive disposition even in his boyhood. Persons intimately acquainted with Dunham all give testimony to the fact that he had a violent temper. He often had terrible fits of rage, during which those who knew him best kept away from fear that he might do them bodily harm.

Ten years ago the Dunham family resided in this city, but James was temporarily employed on a ranch near town. He would occasionally come in and go to his mother for money. When she refused to accede to his demands he would abuse her until she gave in, that she might get rid of him before his rage made him a maniac. Once the mother absolutely refused to be intimidated. Dunham then went into the yard and took revenge by killing his mother's chickens. He seized three of them, one after another, and after wringing their necks literally tore them to pieces.

The buckskin horse which Dunham abandoned yesterday was raised by James K. Wells, one of the murderer's victims, and the animal was Wells' property during the dozen years of its existence up to the time of the tragedy. The horse was very docile, and the girls and children of the neighborhood frequently borrowed it, as *Fashion* (the name given to the animal by Colonel McGlincy) was good either as a saddle or driving horse. Wells thought a great deal of the animal, and the neighbors were wont to remark that Jim Wells and his horse were inseparable.

Newspaper: *San Jose Mercury*
Date: May 30, 1896

The note found in Mrs. Dunham's room and supposed to have been written by her has been pronounced a forgery by C. D. Wright, C.

T. Smith, Undersheriff Benson and others. They carefully compared specimens of the handwriting of both Mrs. Dunham and James Dunham with the card, and the resemblance to the murderer's chirography was very marked. Those who made the comparison came to a unanimous conclusion that Dunham, and not his wife, wrote the note. The murderer's object in forging such a missive is not apparent.

Newspaper: *San Jose Mercury*
Date: May 30, 1896

Dunham apparently has a double. A telephone message was received from Concord, Contra Costa County, yesterday afternoon, stating that a man answering the description of the fugitive murderer, passed through that place at noon, stopping long enough to take dinner. The stranger must bear a remarkable resemblance to Dunham, as the report says the description tallied in almost every respect.

Newspaper: *Campbell Weekly Visitor*
Date: May 30, 1896

The preparations for the funeral of Mr. and Mrs. McGlincy, Mrs. Hattie Dunham, James Wells and Robert Briscoe were begun on Thursday, and late in the evening of that day the bodies were moved from the house to the Congregational Church where the services were to be held under the direction of W. L. Woodrow of San Jose, on Friday afternoon. The hour appointed was 2pm, but by twelve o'clock carriages were seen gathering from all directions and long before the time for the beginning of the services the streets in the vicinity of the church were crowded with vehicles. After all available space was filled in town, the teams were compelled to stop along the principal avenues until long lines of conveyances extended out a considerable distance in every direction. It was probably one of the largest assemblies that ever came together for a similar purpose in California. The instance of five persons, the victims of the murderous hand of a single assassin, being buried at one time from such a quiet and peaceful village is probably without parallel in history. People flocked to witness the scene from all parts of the country. The funeral was conducted under the auspices of the Independent Order of Odd Fellows of which order Colonel McGlincy and James Wells were members. Many of the members of San Jose and Santa Clara lodges were in attendance and Morning Light Lodge of Campbell turned out in a body. All the pall-bearers, of which there were thirty, were Odd Fellows.

The floral offerings were almost innumerable and many of them of most beautiful design. The San Jose Grange presented a piece in the form of an open book with the names "Brother" and "Sister" worked across the pages. The Odd Fellows gave a pillow of roses, two by three feet, at the top of which was inscribed "Vengeance is mine, I will repay saith the Lord." One of the most beautiful and appropriate designs was presented by the Cambrian Literary Society, the piece representing a chair about two and a half feet in height on the back of which was inscribed "Jim." The vacant chair was a mute expression of the sorrow of the Society in the loss of its beloved president, James Wells.

The ceremonies as conducted by Past Grand Master P. F. Gosbey acting as Noble Grand and N. H. Hyland as Chaplain were most impressive. The procession to the cemetery was upwards of three miles in length and not less than 400 carriages taking part. The ritual service of the Lodge was concluded at the cemetery and the caskets deposited side by side in their last resting place. The floral pieces as they were placed upon the graves presented a most beautiful appearance, all the graves being completely covered.

Newspaper: *Sacramento Bee*
Date: May 30, 1896

It is now asserted that James C. Dunham, the fiendish murderer of Santa Clara County, is insane. Then let him be hanged all the quicker.

If the law would be amended so as to absolutely prohibit the plea of insanity as a defense for murder, it would be astonishing how rare the tribe of homicidal lunatics would become.

Newspaper: *San Francisco Chronicle*
Date: May 31, 1896

As the matter is sifted more and more, wonder is expressed that Parker and Snell were afraid to get a crowd and follow the murderer without delay. Those who saw and recognized the murderer, knowing he had committed the crime, seem to have gone asleep immediately after they saw him, for they allowed him to get hours the start without trying to overtake him. Nobody at Smiths Creek seems to have made any effort to apprehend Dunham further than to telephone the news here—then sit before a log fire and discuss the crime.

Newspaper: *San Francisco Chronicle*
Date: May 31, 1896

Charles Quincy, who lives four miles below the new Almaden mines, knows Dunham better than anyone in the country. The murderer and he were schoolmates and have been good friends ever since, Dunham often sleeping with his friend.

"I do not believe Jim is insane," said Quincy today, "but I think something has stirred him deeply. I do not remember anything about him that shows him to have been particularly vindictive. He always spoke calmly, was proud and neat about himself, being a careful dresser. If he held deep and bitter grudges against those he did not like he did not show it by much talk or by threats against people."

Continuing in his description, Quincy said: "The last time I saw Dunham was just before the carnival. He was in San Jose. I know he had not been home very much lately, but do not know just where he lived. I understood from him that he boarded in Santa Clara during the time he was going to school.

"Dunham was of a roving disposition, never remaining anywhere long. One peculiar thing about him was the fact that he would never travel anywhere on cars. He would hitch up a team or go on a bicycle. He once drove as far as Idaho in a cart. There is no man in the country more familiar with trails and roads than Jim Dunham. I think he may have tried to get over to Livermore, for he knows that country well.

"The peculiar thing about Dunham by which I could know him anywhere is his eyes. They are very deep, and on a side view they look very clear blue, as if the pupil were set way back.

"So far as I know Dunham's temper was not violent. If he had trouble with anyone he tried to patch it up and smooth things over without a quarrel. Dunham had trouble with his mother four years ago. He deserted her, came to our house for a few weeks and swore he would never return. But he returned to her before she died.

"Dunham always had plenty of money, was free with it and paid his debts. He did not drink, use tobacco or gamble.

"I have heard Dunham's friends say that the family troubles began about the time he started to Santa Clara College, because the McGlincys wanted his wife to leave him. I have every reason to believe that Hattie Wells married Jim just to spite Charley, his brother, with whom she had quarreled because Charley went with another girl."

Newspaper: *San Jose Mercury*
Date: June 2, 1896

Of all of the persons to endeavor to throw light upon the mystery as to Dunham's motive for the awful crimes he committed there was no one who has yet come forward with information who so nearly solves the mystery as W. H. Johnson, a young man who has recently completed a law course under attorney John Goss and who will take the Supreme Court examination in August.

Mr. Johnson conducts a barbershop on South First Street near San Antonio, but has studied law during spare hours. Attorney Goss was retained by Dunham some weeks ago to foreclosure his mortgage on a property of A. C. Penniman, and this caused Dunham to frequently visit the attorney's office and Mr. Johnson became acquainted with Dunham. From the statements made to a Mercury reporter by Mr. Johnson yesterday it is to be concluded that Dunham is a rational, deep-thinking, unscrupulous villain, whose plans for crime were deeply laid for days before he brought them to the atrocious climax.

"I believe that James Dunham is as sane a man as either you or I," said Johnson yesterday, "and as I think of what he told me weeks ago I am more and more convinced that his plot to murder the McGlincy family was being worked out by him during several weeks and perhaps months.

"On the day of the big parade during the Rose Carnival here Dunham was in Mr. Goss' office in the Minna building, and he and I sat at the window conversing as we were waiting for the procession to come along.

"In that conversation he asked me this question: 'Providing a man marries into a wealthy family and has issue and afterward the entire family should die, would that child inherit the entire estate?'

"I promptly replied, for I had given this subject considerable study, 'it would.'

"He then said: 'Are you sure?' and I remember now that he accented the word 'sure' and looked me straight in the eyes.

"I told him that that was the rule of consanguinity.

"He then said: 'I'm glad of that,' and then covered what he said by the further remark: 'I'm glad of that, as I intend to study law myself and am anxious to learn legal points.'

"From that our conversation drifted into different topics, during which he said he was studying at Santa Clara College, and was taking the classical course with a view of taking up the study of law thereafter.

"I asked him if he was married then. I understood him to say 'No,' but that he intended to be.

"At this juncture the procession arrived and thus concluded our conversation.

"Considering the mode in which he committed the crime, using a silent weapon as far as circumstances would permit, it appears to me that he intended to kill only the members of the family, then depart as though he had not been home, and having been absent two days previous, suspicion would undoubtedly have been cast upon the hired men. But having come in contact with Wells in the struggle between liberty and death, he was compelled to use a boisterous weapon. Then, knowing that he had attracted the attention of the hired men, he concluded to slay them also, and thus cover up all possibilities of detection.

"In talking to me he seemed to speak very rationally, and his actions would indicate that he was a very deliberate man. I knew he intended to study law, and I was not in the least surprised that he asked this question, but little did I think that I was furnishing information upon which Dunham was founding his plot to strike down a whole family."

Mr. Johnson was questioned as to why he had withheld this extremely important information so far, and he explained that he desired to see Mr. Goss before divulging. As a student in Mr. Goss' office he did not believe in telling the conversations held there without consulting his superior, and especially when it was possible, in case of Dunham's capture, it might become Mr. Goss' duty to defend him.

Newspaper: *San Jose Mercury*
Date: June 2, 1896

At the sheriff's office in the city last evening definite information was received that murderer Dunham was seen last Friday at the Coe Ranch, 10 miles south of Indian Gulch.

On the following night he made his appearance at the ranch of James McIlrath, a short distance from the Highland school house.

The information concerning Dunham's movements was brought to San Jose by Wood Wadhams, a resident of Santa Clara. He has for some time been employed upon the Newell Ranch in San Felipe Valley. The owner of this ranch is the teacher of the San Felipe school.

The mail reaches these mountain ranches only semi-occasionally from Evergreen and Madrone. It is usually brought out by one of the ranchers of the neighborhood who may chance to come to the post office. In consequence sometimes a whole week passes without any news being received from the outside world. This happened last week, and nothing concerning the murder at Campbell was known to those who lived upon the Coe and McIlrath Ranches last Friday and Saturday nights when Dunham, driven to desperation by hunger, made his appearance there.

On Sunday morning some papers, among them a Mercury of Friday morning, was brought to the Coe Ranch and Charles Coe, the owner of the place, was astounded to read the account of the chase after Dunham at Smiths Creek and that was when Coe learned of the murder. His interest in the news was increased by the fact that he had seen Dunham on Friday afternoon last.

As Coe told his story Dunham was well known to him, he having worked upon the ranch a few years ago. The fugitive looked like he was worn out with a hard tramp through the brush. His face was scratched—as Coe supposed—by making his way through the brambles on the hillsides. Dunham did not have much to say except that he had been tramping around, and had lost his way in a gulch. He spoke of being very hungry, and asked if he could get some provisions. He was told that he could have some. Dunham then wanted to know if he could buy a rifle. He said he had money and would pay for all he got. It was suggested that if he was so flush he ought to go to Gilroy or Hollister and buy what he wanted.

Dunham persisted in his efforts to make a purchase of a firearm, and Coe showed him a rifle that had been in use some time, and that the owner himself had bought second-hand for $14.

The rifle, with thirty rounds of ammunition, and a sack of provisions were secured by Dunham. He started away in the direction of the McDermitt Ranch, which is in what is known as the Packwood Valley, south of Smiths Creek and east of the Eighteen-Mile House. It is believed the Dunham is in hiding somewhere on this great cattle ranch. It consists of about 17,000 acres, and is owned by James McDermitt, a millionaire of Oakland.

After learning that Dunham had been seen in that vicinity, Wadhams began an investigation, and found fresh footprints of a man upon old trails where men seldom or never go either on foot or horseback. The tracks were not regular, and some of them were blurred as if made by a man who wrapped one of his feet up with clothes while the other print was made by a shoe with a rather narrow toe. The tracks were going and coming as if the man who made them had been back and forth on the trail a great deal.

It was also found that there were bicycle tracks in the level places around the region thereabout. This was considered strange, as a bicycle is seldom seen or ridden in that rough, mountainous region. The bicycle tracks were especially distinct across several bridges in the San Felipe Valley. They had attracted the attention of Wadhams as being strange and unusual before he heard anything about Dunham being in that vicinity or even about the murder and the search that was being made for him.

The tracks were always very wide, as if made by a flat tire or one that was extra-large.

Last Friday night at 12 o'clock Wadhams was on his way home from a dance in the San Felipe schoolhouse. It was bright moonlight, and when he crossed the bridge he looked and made certain that there were not any fresh bicycle tracks upon it. At a very early hour the next morning he had occasion to cross the same bridge and he then distinctly traced the mysterious bicycle tracks. It was evident that the rider had passed by the bridge sometime between midnight and 8 o'clock in the morning.

No traces of this bicycle have since been found, and the officers have no doubt that it is the same one that Dunham has since used in the mountains. How he got the wheel up there at the same time as his horse is a mystery. Some of the officers now believe that he has a confederate, who is also a cycler, and who may have taken the bicycle into the mountains and left it at some prearranged place for Dunham to get and use in case he should need it.

Wadhams knows every trail and gulch and barbed wire fence in the region where Dunham was seen last, and he will be a valuable aid in guiding the searching party.

Newspaper: *San Jose Mercury*
Date: June 2, 1896

The will of Mrs. Ada M. McGlincy was filed for probate yesterday by E. N. Parr, who is named as an executor. Hattie B. Dunham, wife of the murderer, is willed $100 and the rest is bequeathed to James K. Wells, her brother.

The petition states that Mrs. McGlincy was 54 years of age, and places the value of the orchard properties in Campbell at $30,000. The place brought in an annual income of $1500. The personal property, farming implements and livestock are valued at $1000. The whole estate was the personal property of the decedent.

The will, which is dated March 7, 1896, names James K. Wells and E. N. Parr as the executors. Wells was the victim of the tragedy, and

Parr consents to act. The next of kin and sole heir is stated to be the infant son of James C. Dunham, which has been adopted by M. T. Brewer of San Francisco. The baby heir is just four weeks old.

The following is the text of the will:

> *First, I give and bequeath to my daughter, Hattie B. Wells (now Hattie B. Dunham, wife of James C. Dunham of the said county of Santa Clara), the sum of one hundred dollars.*
>
> *Secondly, I give and bequeath all the rest, residue and remainder of my personal and real estate and all property of whatsoever kind or nature owned by me at the time of my death to my son, James K. Wells, of the said county and State.*
>
> *Thirdly, I have purposely omitted to bequeath any of my estate to my kind husband, and it is my will that he shall not receive any portion of my estate. I believe that my husband will agree that the distribution of my estate as herein bequeathed is made with the best and purest of motive, and for the best interest of my children and beloved husband.*
>
> *Lastly, I hereby nominate and appoint my son James K. Wells and E. N. Parr of Campbell as the executors of my last will and testament, and I direct that they be not required to give bonds as such for any purpose, and hereby revoke all former wills by me made.*

Newspaper: *San Jose Mercury*
Date: June 2, 1896

Edward D'Oyly, was a schoolmate of Dunham's at the Washburn School. D'Oyly was seen last night by a Mercury representative, and said: "I went to school with the murderer for about a month, and used to sit next to him. He seemed quite studious, but the boys at the school always noticed that he never wore shoes that were mates. In the morning when Dunham would come to school we would at once glance at his feet, and would always see one shoe with a pointed toe and the other either square- or round-pointed. They were all apparently the same size and in good condition. When he saw us noticing his feet he would show little embarrassment. We 'joshed' him, but he never got mad."

It is probable that Dunham had on shoes that were not mates when he went into the mountains, as he tied the left one up in a sack, thinking to avoid identification.

Newspaper: *San Jose Mercury*
Date: June 2, 1896

ELGIN, ILLINOIS - The news of Colonel McGlincy's murder was first announced to the Elgin public by a bulletin posted in front of the *News-Advocate* block. The affair is a shocking surprise to his numerous friends and acquaintances here.

Colonel McGlincy was born in Shepherdstown, Jefferson County, West Virginia, May 21, 1840. In July, 1868, he and his wife came west and located in Chicago. In the following March they moved to Elgin, the Colonel becoming daily editor of the Elgin *Gazette*, which position he continued to hold after the *Gazette* became merged with the Elgin *Advocate*.

His first wife, who now resides at 543 Chicago Street, was Miss Asenath R. Welles. They were married in West Virginia in July, 1868, a few days before their removal west. She is nearly prostrated with grief at the sad affair.

Deceased leaves no relatives in Illinois, but his mother, a brother and three sisters reside near Harpers Ferry, or did a very short time ago.

Colonel McGlincy is remembered most kindly by nearly all old residents of Elgin. He was a typical Southerner, whole-souled and generous, making friends with nearly everyone. He was very prominent in dairy circles and no dairy convention was complete without an address from him. From May, 1877, until the same month of 1887, exactly ten years, he was Secretary of the Elgin Board of Trade. He had also been Secretary of the Northwestern Dairymen's Association and Secretary of the State Dairymen's Association.

He served with distinction all through the Civil War, and part of the time fought under Stonewall Jackson. He was prominent among the Odd Fellows and held the position of District Deputy Grand Master for a number of years. While in Elgin he was a member of the Kane Lodge, No. 47, I. O. O. F.

Newspaper: *San Francisco Chronicle*
Date: June 2, 1896

The businessmen of San Jose were surprised this afternoon to receive a mysterious communication. About the middle of the afternoon special messenger boys went from door to door of all residences of respectable citizens leaving a plainly addressed envelope, in which was a neatly printed circular, which reads as follows:

> San Jose, June 2 – Dear Sir: *This invitation and notice is given because of the confidence reposed in you that its contents will not be divulged. The scene of the most heartless crimes of history has been laid in our county near our own homes. James C. Dunham has foully murdered three women and three men. The murderer is at liberty, with the chances strongly in favor of his escape. The laws of our State offer no substantial aid in bringing about his capture. Believing it to be the wish of every citizen to aid in supporting the laws of the land, and when the law is inadequate, to heroically come to its support, you are appealed to by a committee to meet in company with many of the best citizens at the Courthouse in the courtroom Department 1, this (Monday) evening, June 1st at 8 o'clock sharp, for the purpose of devising ways and means for assisting in the work of pursuing and capturing the murderer, James C. Dunham.*

Be assured that this meeting is not called for the purpose of forming a vigilance committee, but solely for the purpose of lawfully assisting the officers and the law in bringing to justice the most vicious criminal in the history of this country. You have the privilege of bringing with you any responsible citizen who will assist, providing that you, as a man of honor, will vouch for his responsibility. Present this notice at the inner door of the courtroom of Department 1.

As this is an occasion and cause that appeals to the heart and manhood of every honorable citizen, we sincerely hope that you will not permit any other matter to interfere whereby you will be unable to attend this meeting.

Respectfully yours,

Committee of Safety.

The response of the circular was that a strong and representative body of men met in the courtroom. At first it was decided to hold the meeting with closed doors, but toward the latter part of the meeting the doors were opened and not so much secrecy observed, though only prominent people were admitted. The meeting showed pretty well the state of the public mind, which is very much excited at present. In fact, it is so much so that it was quite a while before the ideas of those present could be so harmonized, that business could be proceeded with.

Notwithstanding that Sheriff Lyndon has worked night and day since the murder, he is blamed because Dunham escaped from Indian Gulch, and his political enemies are taking advantage of public feeling. He is blamed because his deputies have been charged, with himself, of having mismanaged the opening of the campaign. The Supervisors of the county are also blamed by some for not offering a reward. As they do not like to shoulder the responsibility of paying a reward, having no legal right to do so, considerable feeling was shown at the meeting. When the meeting drew to its close it was decided for one thing to raise as much money by public subscription as possible, the money so subscribed to be offered as an additional reward.

The Chairman spoke of the object of the meeting, saying that the reputation of Santa Clara County was now at stake. Not long ago a woman had been murdered in a lodging house, and no clue to the murderer had been found. Now a family was almost obliterated, and the murderer must be caught.

Newspaper: *San Francisco Chronicle*
Date: June 2, 1896

M. T. Brewer applied yesterday to be appointed guardian of Percy Osborn Dunham, the only survivor of the terrible massacre enacted at the McGlincy homestead near San Jose. The petition recites the fact of the murder, charges Dunham with the killing and declares that Dunham is now either dead or a fugitive from justice. Brewer is grand-uncle of the child and the little one is now domiciled with him at his home, 729 Turk Street.

"Baby" Dunham has not suffered any from its change of climate and diet. It sleeps the hours away like any well-regulated infant should who has less than four weeks to its credit. It cries just often enough to prove the healthful condition of his lungs.

An heir to an imperial throne is not guarded more carefully than this babe whose heritage of misfortune opens to him the hearts of all.

A stalwart policeman guards the Brewer home day and night. He is housed from wind and weather and keeps his vigil in the front room, the parlor of this comfortable, substantial home. While Dunham's whereabouts are unknown the law will shield the babe and its protectors from any possible attack.

Newspaper: *San Jose Mercury*
Date: June 3, 1896

The story of Wood Wadhams, of Dunham having been on Coe and McIlrath Ranches, proved to be a fake. The posse which went out to investigate returned at 7:45 o'clock yesterday morning much disgusted.

"It must be acknowledged that young Wadhams of Santa Clara completely deceived the officers with his story Monday night," said Undersheriff Benson last evening in an interview with the Mercury representative. "When Wadhams was brought to San Jose by Marshall Lovell of Santa Clara I questioned him closely. I took down what he said in writing and cross-questioned him upon the various details of how Dunham had been seen at the Coe and McIlrath Ranches. He could not be caught in any point, however, there being no contradiction that could be discovered, and naturally Sheriff Lyndon and myself began to believe there was something in the story. After we had got some distance on the road to Evergreen, Wadhams began to oppose our intention of going to the Coe and McIrath Ranches to verify his story. He said that there was no use in going there as Dunham had been at those points two or three days before and it would be a loss of time. He said the best thing that could be done would be to start on the trail on Pine Ridge through the McDermitt Ranch. We were determined before beginning a long hard chase to verify what Wadhams had told us, and we kept heading for Coe's place. Then he deliberately began an attempt to mislead us in giving directions as to where Coe lived. He could have accomplished this purpose, but several of the rest of us had a good idea of the place. Then Wadhams said there was no use in going there, as Coe was not at home.

"We went by way of Evergreen into the San Felipe Valley. Our first stop was made at the Rathbone Ranch, about eighteen miles from San Jose. We've reached there about 4 o'clock in the morning. The people at this place had heard nothing of traces of Dunham having

been seen in that vicinity. This did not disconcert Wadhams and he made quite a hero of himself around the place. It is believed that this is due to the fact that Wadhams was sweet upon a pretty girl who lived there. It was then learned definitely that Wadhams had attempted to give the wrong direction as to Coe's house, and it was also learned where James McIlrath lived. After drinking some coffee and eating a bite we started out for McIlrath's. There the statement that there had been no knowledge of the murderer in that neighborhood till last Sunday was also disproved. Wadhams did not appear to be much disconcerted when he was thus exposed, but he had no desire to go with the party to the Coe place. He gladly took charge of the team at a point where it was not convenient to go further with the rig. Charles Coe denied the whole story. He said he had not sold a rifle, ammunition and provisions to anyone. This settled the matter and we started on our return. We picked up Wadhams and brought him back to town, but it was not with a very good grace. He did not have much to say on the return trip. I cannot imagine what was the young man's object in spinning such a yarn," said Undersheriff Benson in conclusion, "unless it was to make a town hero of himself at Santa Clara. He also probably thought it would be a fine scheme if it would enable him to head a posse as a guide in search of the murderer through the mountains. If we had been taken up the trail instead of investigating his story we would have been good for a two or three days' exciting chase through the mountains at least."
Wadhams, when seen at Santa Clara by a Mercury reporter, declared his story was true and expressed his intention of leaving Santa Clara again last night for the San Felipe Valley and take up the search from where he alleges he saw the bicycle tracks, through the Chicopee Pass into the San Joaquin. He announced that he believed Dunham would take this route, but would make slow time, as he would avoid the main roads and has not the endurance to climb hills very rapidly. "I will go fully armed and equipped with provisions to stay in that country for some time," said Wadhams. "I know the country and can camp anywhere, using my saddle for a pillow and my horse blanket for bed. I have done this before and will do it until Dunham is caught

or has skipped from that part of the country." Wadhams said he expected B. Van Horn to accompany him upon the expedition.

Newspaper: *San Jose Mercury*
Date: June 3, 1896

Constable Ed Healey and Deputy Sheriff James Edwards returned to San Jose about 11 o'clock last night from Las Animas Valley. Yesterday morning at 11:30 o'clock he received a telephone message from Charles Marcine of that place stating that a person supposed to be Dunham was seen in that locality Monday night. The officers went at once to the Roper Ranch, between Las Animas and San Felipe and about fourteen miles east of Evergreen.

Mrs. Roper, who the officers pronounce to be a cool and level-headed woman, told them that Monday morning her eight-year-old son had informed her that he saw a man with sacks tied round his feet crawling under the bushes across the creek opposite the house. Monday night her six-year-old son said he heard voices from across the creek. She went out and listened and heard the voices. She called another lady who was in the house and she also heard the voices distinctly. Mrs. Roper's husband was in San Jose, but she notified two Swede wood-choppers on the place and Marcine, who lives nearby, of the occurrence and these three went over to search the place from which the voices came. They could see nothing that night, but yesterday morning they found where a man had been sitting and had left a piece of orange peel. They traced large tracks in the wet grass for some distance up the ridge.

The officers, and assisted by Marcine, endeavored to find the tracks yesterday afternoon, but could not, as the grass had dried. After searching for four hours the officers returned to town, as Constable Haley has a sale this morning at which he has to be present, but the reports made such an impression upon him that he will return to the place and renew the search this afternoon. Haley states that Marcine is certain the man seen and heard was Dunham.

Newspaper: *San Jose Mercury*
Date: June 4, 1896

The Citizens' Executive Committee entered upon its duties with energy and determination yesterday morning. The entire day was devoted to outlining the ways and means for securing a fund a $10,000 to be offered as a reward for the capture of James C. Dunham dead or alive.

The Committee also decided that the cooperation of the ladies at the county in the matter of raising funds for the reward was indispensable and the following circular letter was issued and sent to a large number of the most prominent ladies of the city.

San Jose, June 3, 1896

Dear Madam: For the first time in the history of this State women are appealed to in a cause the like of which they have never before been asked to aid.

Three of your sex have been most cruelly murdered, and we desire the material assistance of every woman in Santa Clara County in bringing the murderer, James C. Dunham to justice. You are asked to assist in this matter to the extent of obtaining subscriptions to complete the sum of ten thousand dollars that is offered by the citizens of Santa Clara County as a reward for the capture of Dunham, dead or alive.

You are earnestly requested to meet with other ladies in the parlors of the Saint James Hotel (near the Court House) Thursday, June 4, at 10:00 AM, then and there to devise a way to canvass the city and county for subscriptions.

Be so good as to not allow any other business to prevent you from attending this meeting.

Respectfully yours,

Citizens' Executive Committee.

Mitchell Phillips of the Committee informed a Mercury reporter that about $3000 of the $10,000 desired was in sight, and he was confident the entire amount would be raised in a short time.

The office of the Committee was besieged yesterday by men seeking engagements to go upon the hunt for Dunham. The Chairman of the Committee informed them that he had no authority to engage anyone to prosecute the search, only to raise subscriptions to pay the reward if he was captured.

Chairman Hyland stated that many men were anxious to go upon the hunt on their own account provided they could secure saddle horses. He desired all who could contribute the use of saddle horses to notify him in order that those restrained from joining the search on this account could secure the same. "Of course," he stated, "these horses will not be given to any but responsible parties."

Newspaper: *San Jose Mercury*
Date: June 4, 1896

Undersheriff S. G. Benson yesterday morning detailed Byron Cottle to go to the McGlincy Ranch and get the old family dog. It is stated that this dog was a pet with Dunham and his only friend upon the place. Cottle left yesterday morning with the dog for Smiths Creek, where he will be used to search Indian Gulch. Many persons are of the opinion that Dunham's dead body lies in this gulch, and out of respect for their wishes this dog will be used in making the last search. It is thought that if anything could find the supposed dead body this dog, who would not desert his friend because he was a murderer, could do it. The Undersheriff has no idea if the search will be productive of any result.

Constable Reynolds of Los Gatos will superintend the search.

Newspaper: *Sacramento Bee*
Date: June 4, 1896

LOS BANOS – Reports still locate Dunham in this vicinity. Local officers are on the alert, and his trail in a southward direction would indicate that he is making for the plains. He would probably reach the river about Firebaugh.

At Tim O'Connor's place about twelve miles northwest of Bell's Station, there was found a freshly-killed calf. A little further on searchers came across a lunch basket, in which was part of the fresh meat. Yesterday a man answering to Dunham's description was seen at the ranch of Chas. Jones, on Los Banos Creek, about fourteen miles from town. He made a raid on the garden, taking all the ripe peas and turnips.

Newspaper: *San Jose Mercury*
Date: June 5, 1896

Mrs. M. T. Brewer, the sister of Mrs. R. P. McGlincy, on last Monday filed a petition in Judge Slack's court in San Francisco to be allowed to adopt the baby boy of James C. Dunham. Next Monday was set as the time for hearing the petition and Judge Slack ordered that the brother and sister of the murderer be notified of the action.

A bodyguard constantly attends the baby and will be maintained until the father is captured and all possibility of his making an effort to secure possession of the child is lost. The child will be named Percy Osborn Brewer, unless some legal technicality regarding its inheritance arises.

Newspaper: *San Jose Mercury*
Date: June 6, 1896

New placards containing announcements of the rewards offered for the arrest of Dunham and two photographs of the murderer were issued yesterday by the Citizens' Executive Committee.

One of the pictures is the same as that sent out by the Sheriff and which has been generally copied by the papers. This was taken in 1894 and presents Dunham as he looked at the time of his marriage to Miss Hattie Wells. The other was taken in 1889, and represents Dunham as he appeared at that time in the rough attire of a ranch hand. This last photograph was found in an old trunk of Dunham's mother. This likeness is in strong contrast to the one subsequently taken, but it is thought the picture will give a good idea of how Dunham will look after securing a change of clothes in the mountains, which it is thought he will probably endeavor to do. In the picture of 1889 Dunham did not have a mustache and his features present a much harder appearance than in the last photograph.

Newspaper: *San Jose Mercury*
Date: June 6, 1896

M. T. Brewer of San Francisco applied yesterday for letters of administration on the estate of his nephew, James K. Wells, one of Dunham's victims. Wells was the son of Mrs. McGlincy by a former marriage and was bequeathed her estate, valued at $30,000. Mr. Brewer also opposes the petition of J. K. Secord for appointment as administrator. He claims that as he has been appointed guardian of Percy Osborne Dunham, the four weeks' old son of the murderer, to whom all the property will descend, he is the proper person to be appointed administrator.

Newspaper: *San Jose Mercury*
Date: June 6, 1896

Byron Cottle returned from Smiths Creek yesterday morning with the McGlincy dog, which had been assisting in the search for any trace of Dunham's body in Indian Gulch. Cottle claims that the idea in many people's minds that Dunham is dead or maimed in Indian Gulch is absurd, but that the search was made with a dog that was Dunham's friend to satisfy all that Dunham had left that vicinity.

Newspaper: *Sacramento Bee*
Date: June 6, 1896

The women of San Jose are thoroughly in earnest in their purpose to make James C. Dunham pay the penalty for his awful crimes. The leaders of the Committee of Safety met again yesterday to discuss the changes that a day had made in the situation and to report the progress of the movement to enlist the support, not only of the women of Santa Clara County, but of the State.

Women have gone from house to house in San Jose, among the rich and the poor, and everywhere there is applause for the Committee of Safety and the heartiest wishes for its welfare. Out on the roads leading from the city to the smaller communities and to the isolated homes of farmers, other women have gone to learn the feeling and to listen to the promises that the mistress of the household will give aid, as far as her means will allow, and will contribute whatever personal work and direction may be found useful in the crusade.

The leaders of the Committee, women who have made their individuality felt in society, fraternal and charitable undertakings, have been quick to understand their own purposes and to outline their own plans. They have no word of disparagement for the efforts of the local authorities in the stern chase over the mountains and in dangerous retreats in the hills. Everything that has been done receives full recognition, but the fact remains that Dunham is still at large, with the power, and perhaps the purpose, to bring ruin to other homes.

They want the men to assume a more personal responsibility for the capture of the murderer and not to leave all effort to the small body of municipal authorities. These women wish to see offered a reward large enough to tempt daring men to risk their lives in an endeavor to bring Dunham into San Jose, dead or alive. And these women roused to a pitch of excitement without parallel in the history of this city, are frank enough to say they would rather see James C. Dunham brought back dead.

An effort will now be made to increase the reward for the capture of Dunham to $20,000. They will themselves contribute as far as their purses will permit. They will ask for contributions from men and women. They will seek assistance from civic and semi-public societies interested in the welfare of the city and county. This money, which will be secured if determined and systematic effort be of any value, will be used to employ man-hunters who know the trails from actual experience.

After the adjournment of the meeting Mrs. Secord, who is the wife of the coroner and a most vigorous promoter of the Committee of Safety, and who withal is a woman who speaks her mind freely upon all occasions, declared vigorously that she wanted to see Dunham captured and punished for his crimes.

"I would be willing to lend a hand to pull the rope, and would be glad of the opportunity," she said. "How he shall be caught is a question to answer. We women know nothing about hunting criminals, but we will raise money to reward any man who will bring him back."

Newspaper: *San Jose Mercury*
Date: June 8, 1896

Tired, sore, discouraged, but still determined, Sheriff Lyndon returned yesterday afternoon after a most trying trip in search of murder Dunham.

Sheriff Lyndon left San Jose Tuesday morning, which was the day after the completion of the search of Smiths Creek, for the mountains east of Hollister, to endeavor to cut off the fugitive in his supposed flight south, and although the Sheriff and his party were unable to strike a clue, they stayed with the search until they were fully satisfied that if Dunham should be laying low, waiting for a decline in the vigilance of the officers as a time for escape, they had the people so thoroughly posted in the mountains that word will be sent to the Sheriff's office as soon as the criminal shows himself in the localities they have visited.

"We've gained but little information of service to us," said Sheriff Lyndon yesterday soon after his arrival on the 5 o'clock afternoon train from Monterey. "We did not strike his trail at any place, and from all we could learn it seems that he could not have passed through the mountains there without being seen and identified."

Newspaper: *San Jose Mercury*
Date: June 8, 1896

The fact that Coroner Secord was seen near Smiths Creek yesterday morning furnished the embryo for a rumor which became widespread yesterday to the effect that murderer Dunham's body had been discovered in Indian Gulch and the Coroner had called to hold an inquest. The fact was that Coroner Secord went to Smiths Creek Wednesday morning to join his family in an outing for two days.

Newspaper: *San Jose Mercury*
Date: June 9, 1896

CHICO - The history of James Dunham, the Santa Clara murderer, in Chico is not one that a respectable citizen would be proud of. Of those who became acquainted with Dunham during his stay in this vicinity, none knew him better than Fred Ackerman, a rancher, who, in the spring of 1893, hired Dunham as a laborer, afterward taking him as a partner in the nursery business.

During the first two or three months of his labor for Ackerman, Dunham was very agreeable and he and Ackerman got along well together. Dunham seldom talked about himself or his relatives, but one day he became confidential and told Ackerman that his father had killed a man and buried him on a ranch either in San Diego or Santa Barbara County, and that he had made such an artistic job of it that no one would be any the wiser or ever find out. As Dunham became better acquainted his demeanor changed. His first offense in Chico was when, at one time, he went to Ackerman and told him that if he would discharge one of his chore men he would obtain for him an industrious young man of good character who would do the work for $5 a month less. This was agreed to and Dunham brought to the ranch a man whom he introduced as "Jim," not giving his other name, and it was not learned until the month was nearly up that "Jim" was his brother. Dunham at first denied the relationship, but afterwards had to admit it.

Mrs. Ackerman often complained to her husband of Dunham's actions. Dunham was very disrespectful and impudent and she was afraid of him. Things went from bad to worse until Dunham and Ackerman became involved in controversy on account of some trees. Ackerman, not liking the way Dunham had been conducting the nursery, told him so, and was threatened by the partner. Soon afterward Ackerman went to the barn to saddle a horse. He had saddled the animal and about to mount when someone pounced upon him from behind and knocked him down. It was Dunham. Being nearly 60 years old, Ackerman was no match for his adversary, who was young and strong. Dunham grasped the old man by the throat with one hand, holding the other over his mouth to prevent an outcry. Dunham then began to twist Ackerman's head in an attempt to break his neck, but Ackerman struggled hard for his life and succeeded in crying out. His scream was heard by one of the man on the ranch, who came to the rescue and pulled Dunham from his victim, who was so exhausted that he had to be helped to the house.

Dunham told some of the men that he wished he had finished Ackerman before help arrived, and that it would have been an easy matter to have claimed that Ackerman met his death from falling from the hay mow and breaking his neck.

Dunham was then discharged and afterward employed by Z. W. Burnham, who owns an orange orchard in the foothills near here. At this place he was employed for short time only, as he soon quarreled with the foreman of the orchard. After leaving Burnham all trace of Dunham was lost.

Dunham went by the name of "Sweet Potato Jim." The origin of the cognomen is not known, but it is known that Dunham was very peculiar in his eating, and while here would eat no light bread, but would make a full meal on corn bread or vegetables.

It is significant as proving Dunham's intent to murder Ackerman that he killed Mrs. Dunham by twisting her head until her neck was broken. In the case of the rancher, fortunately, this means failed.

Newspaper: *San Jose Mercury*
Date: June 9, 1896

A letter addressed to the Postmaster at the Campbell Post Office from Mrs. Virginia McGlincy of Washington, D. C., brings to light another of the very sad features of the late tragedy. The letter states that Mr. McGlincy's mother, brother and three sisters in Washington were almost crazed with grief when the news reached them on the night of May 28th, the second day after the murder. The first information came to them through a newspaper dispatch, and the shock almost drove them wild. They had received a letter from the Colonel only two days before, telling of the bicycle accident in which James Wells was injured and of the birth of the grandchild, and little thought that on the evening of that very day the writer would be struck down in cold blood by the father of the baby spoken of. The mother of Mr. McGlincy is now 86 years old, and, as she is in feeble health, it is feared that she cannot survive the terrible shock.

Newspaper: *San Jose Mercury*
Date: June 11, 1896

SAN LUIS OBISPO - A search in this vicinity for murderer Dunham, the destroyer of the McGlincy family at Campbell, has resolved itself into a pursuit of the escaped outlaw Phillip Crowley. It was Crowley and not Dunham who stopped a woman on the road near San Miguel yesterday and begged for food, and later dined at the home of a rancher.

When Sheriff Ballou was apprised of the presence of a stranger in the hills near San Miguel, he gave the matter considerable thought in a short space of time and concluded that the description of the man met on the road near San Miguel might fit someone else other than Dunham.

He took a photograph of Dunham and one of Crowley and started for San Miguel. He at once visited the woman who had been halted and showed to her of the photographs. She recognized Crowley's picture as that of the man who had begged for something to eat from her. She positively identified the picture of Crowley.

Newspaper: *San Jose Mercury*
Date: June 12, 1896

Wood Wadhams of Santa Clara, who led the officers on a wild goose chase to San Felipe Valley by stating that Dunham had been there and had secured a gun and cartridges a Charley Coe's place, has secured affidavits to show that he was not wholly to blame.

Newspaper: *San Jose Mercury*
Date: June 13, 1896

MAMMOTH TANK - Murderer Dunham is now across the Mexican border, secure from pursuit. He was seen in this oasis of the desert over a week ago, and has had plenty of time to make his way to the boundary and across.

The person who saw Dunham is a Southern Pacific employee, well known to Southern California railroad men. He is opposed to what he considers unpleasant notoriety in connection with the case and would consent to give a complete account of his encounter with the Campbell butcher only on a pledge that his name should not be used in connection with the story. However, he is ready to give the authorities all the information in his possession.

Newspaper: *San Jose Mercury*
Date: June 13, 1896

The officers in this city when interviewed last night did not place much reliance in the above story from Mammoth Tank, but by means of telegrams an attempt will be made to head the murderer off in case he has reached the Mexican border or beyond.

Newspaper: *San Jose Mercury*
Date: June 13, 1896

At a late hour last night a report came from Santa Clara to the effect that a man supposed to be Dunham had been chased out of the vacant house on Washington Street. It is known as the Arguello House, but has been unoccupied for some time. Shortly before 12 o'clock last night a party went to the house on an investigation, taking with them some unsuspecting individuals with the intention of having some fun with them. After the house was reached a man ran out. He disappeared in the darkness, while a shot was fired to make the affair more real, so that the parties who were not in on the hoax became very much excited. Deputy Sheriff Menton soon heard of the affair, and was very indignant at the attempt to joke about so serious a matter. The officer threatened to arrest some of the parties to the hoax.

Newspaper: *San Jose Mercury*
Date: June 17, 1896

The public interest in the chase of James C. Dunham, the murderer of the McGlincy family, continues unabated, and all sorts of stories are brought or sent to the Sheriff's office every day. In accordance with the plan adopted by Sheriff Lyndon every rumor is investigated. The usual result is that the stories are found to be based on imagination, but in the hope that the right trail may be struck at any moment nothing is overlooked.

Newspaper: *San Jose Mercury*
Date: June 13, 1896

A damage suit will be instituted in the Superior Court today in which James C. Dunham, the fugitive murderer, will be cited to appear as a defendant. The action is to be brought by Dr. Jacob A. Shesler and Elizabeth Shesler, the aged parents of Minnie Shesler, the servant girl who was one of Dunham's victims. The amount for which judgment is asked is $25,000.

The Sheslers claim that they were almost wholly dependent upon their daughter Minnie for support. She aided them in securing the necessaries of life, and was paying the interest on the mortgage on the Shesler home. Since her death the family have suffered greatly, and are now faced with the danger that the home may be sold under foreclosure proceedings.

As far as can be learned all the property that Dunham possesses is a note and mortgage for $1400 against the Penniman Fruit Company. Service of summons will be made on Dunham if he is arrested while the case is pending. If he remains at large the Sheslers expect a judgment by default. In this case the mortgage will go to them as judgment debtors.

Newspaper: *San Jose Mercury*
Date: June 20, 1896

The contest over the estate of James K. Wells, deceased, came up before Judge Reynolds yesterday. Public Administrator J. K. Secord asked for letters, as also did M. T. Brewer, guardian of the infant son of James C. Dunham.

The question at issue was to whether Dunham killed Mrs. McGlincy or James K. Wells first. Brewer contended that Mrs. McGlincy died first, and by reason of his relationship he should have control of the child's estate. Circumstantial evidence as to Mrs. McGlincy's prior death was offered and not contradicted.

The matter was taken under advisement, the Court only announcing that the administrator's bond would be $3500.

Newspaper: *San Jose Mercury*
Date: June 22, 1896

Sheriff Lyndon and Undersheriff Benson visited the McGlincy Ranch yesterday afternoon on a tour of inspection in search of further details regarding the murder of the McGlincy family by James C. Dunham. The only important piece of evidence found relating to the case was a summary in the handwriting of Mrs. McGlincy of Dunham's misconduct to her daughter, his wife. This document was written on seven sheets of scrap paper and appeared to be the result of roughly jotting down various incidents from time to time as they would occur to her. Each incident was carefully dated and was apparently being formulated for the purpose of furnishing evidence of cruelty in a contemplated divorce proceeding. The document repeatedly referred to Dunham's ill nature in a general way, and stated that since 9 January, when they came to the McGlincy Ranch to live, he had never been known to speak a pleasant word to his wife in the presence of the family.

It recited the statement of Mrs. Dunham that while in Sacramento she accompanied her husband to a lodging house in search of rooms, where he left her and failed to return. She went back to her old lodgings and waited until midnight for him in the hall, but he failed to put in an appearance that night, and she sought a bed from the landlady. She (Mrs. Dunham) thought her husband was drinking and gambling at the time.

It was stated that Mrs. Dunham had to beg for every dime given her. On one occasion he abused her severely because she asked him to assist her in preparing mushrooms for supper.

The record seemed incomplete, but officers considered it valuable in showing the relationship between Dunham and the family which he murdered.

Sheriff Lyndon stated yesterday that he had received no new clew regarding the whereabouts of Dunham. He still believes the murderer to be in hiding in the mountains that border this county and that his place of concealment will be divulged soon.

Newspaper: *San Francisco Chronicle*
Date: June 28, 1896

Judge Reynolds has decided that M. T. Brewer, guardian of the infant son of murderer James C. Dunham, is entitled to letters of administration on the estate of the late James K. Wells. Public Administrator J. K. Secord had also applied for letters and the question at issue was whether Dunham killed Mrs. McGlincy or James Wells first.

The court decided that the weight of evidence showed that Mrs. McGlincy died first and therefore Mr. Brewer by reason of his relationship should have control over the child's estate. Brewer is, therefore, appointed as administrator and his bond was fixed at $3500.

Newspaper: *San Francisco Chronicle*
Date: July 8, 1896

SAN DIEGO - Charles Dunham, a brother of James Dunham, the murderer, has been here for the past few days and has gone to his ranch near Dulzura in this county. Dunham intends to rent this property and then return to his home at San Jose. He has so far declined to discuss the great crime committed by his brother. Both are well known here.

They were here when their father died and was buried. The ranch which Charles has now gone to visit was formerly owned and occupied by his father. Many people here believe the murderer would naturally steer for this section and lower California on account of his knowledge of the country.

Newspaper: *San Jose Mercury*
Date: July 22, 1896

A man who is suspected of being Dunham, the Campbell murderer, is being held for identification by the Mexican authorities at Jolapa, State of Vera Cruz. Sheriff Lyndon received intelligence concerning the suspect on the 13th inst. and immediately telegraphed to the American Legation at the City of Mexico for photograph and particulars. Yesterday he received the following letter been reply:

Mexico, July 15, 1896

Dear Sir: Your telegram of the 13th has been received, I have requested the Mexican authorities to furnish me with photographs of the presumed Dunham. The facts reported to this Legation by the Foreign Office in reference to the man are as follows: An American was arrested for disorderly conduct at Jolapa, State of Vera Cruz, and gave his name as John S. Kittrell, but a Mexican woman, the mistress of the man, stated to the authorities that the name given was not his true name, and that he had confessed to her that he had committed several murders in the United States. Some time previously the authorities had received from you a description of Dunham with photographs taken in 1889 and 1895. The detectives find a striking resemblance between the man in jail and the photographs, and they say that other individual signs given by you coincide with those found upon the man arrested. I have requested the authorities to hold the man if possible, under the charge already made against him, till he could be identified from California. It might be well for you to provide yourself with proper extradition papers, or for you to come immediately to identify the party. The Department of State at Washington might be requested through the proper channel to have the man held awaiting extradition papers. You will no doubt take such steps as to lose no time in identifying the party and asking for his provisional arrest under the extradition law.

Yours truly,

Y. Sepulveda

"Charge d'Affairs ad interim"

The sheriff will telegraph the authorities at Jolapa to send a photograph of the prisoner at once. Until this and a detailed description of the man are received nothing further can be done.

Newspaper: *San Francisco Chronicle*
Date: August 29, 1896

Judge Reynolds today made an order allowing $40 a month out of the estate of Mrs. Ada McGlincy for the support of Percy Osborn Brewer, the infant son of the late Mrs. Hattie B. Dunham. Letters of administration on the estate of Mrs. Dunham were also granted M. T. Brewer, and the personal property belonging to the estate of James K. Wells, another of the murdered family, was ordered sold.

Newspaper: *San Jose Mercury*
Date: January 7, 1897

OREGON CITY, OR. - John W. C. Green, who has been hiding in this city for the past two days, having deserted the British ship *Lord Elgin*, which left Portland for Cape Town last week, tells a seemingly probable story of the escape from this country of James C. Dunham, who murdered the McGlincys near San Jose, on this 27th of last May.

Green says that in April and May he worked on the ranch of Bernard D. Murphy near San Jose, and during a part of that time Dunham was a fellow laborer with him on the ranch. At the end of May Green went to San Francisco and stopped at Peter McManus' boarding house, but shipped on June 5th as Second Officer to the American ship *Saint John* with a full cargo of wheat and flour for New York.

When seven days out, while the vessel was off the Mexican coast, a stowaway showed up on deck and Green recognized him as Dunham.

Dunham appealed to Green not to reveal his identity, to call him Brown and treat him well, and gave the officer $80 in gold. At the mate's request the stowaway was assigned to his watch and put to work as a seaman. The *Saint John* had a rather slow passage and did not arrive at New York until November 17th. Green and Dunham went ashore together and near the wharf met an officer of the filibustering ship *Bermuda*. The idea of volunteering greatly pleased Dunham, and he at once made arrangements to go to Cuba. The vessel left port the next day and Dunham went with it.

Green claims that was the last he saw of the murderer, whom he did not then know to be a murderer. In explanation of his ignorance of the McGlincy massacre, Green says he seldom looks at a newspaper, being addicted to novel reading to such a degree that all his spare time is thus employed.

Dunham at first supposed that Green knew why he was traveling as a stowaway and talked to him about the murder. When he found that the mate had heard nothing about the affair he turned it off as a joke and said he was making the trip for the sake of adventure.

In New York Green says he happened to run across an old advertisement for Dunham, and then he looked up a newspaper file in a waterfront saloon and learned all about the matter. He went overland to San Francisco and then immediately to Portland. Dunham professed to be entirely ignorant of the work of a sailor, but Green said that hardly could be true, for the third time he was sent up he could furl a royal or a gallant as well as anybody. He was regarded as a most reliable lookout on the ship. He was active and quick to learn and made an excellent sailor.

Green represents himself as a graduate of the University of Virginia, class of '86, and his writing and language do not contradict the claim.

He says he has followed the sea off and on for more than four years, mostly on the Pacific, and his weather-worn appearance bears out the assertion. He is now 28 years old. His parents, he says, live in San Francisco, his father being in the drug business. He swears his story is true, and there is no way either to prove or disprove it here. Green left for San Francisco tonight.

Newspaper: *San Francisco Chronicle*
Date: February 5, 1898

Minnie Shesler, the daughter of Jacob Shesler, was murdered by James C. Dunham when he destroyed the McGlincy family, near Campbell, nearly two years ago. She was the maid of Mrs. Dunham and was butchered with her mistress.

Some months after the bloody deed Jacob Shesler sued James C. Dunham for damages for the loss of the services of his daughter and only child, he being old and infirm and depending largely upon her. He secured judgment for $8000. When the writ of execution came to the Sheriff he could find no property but securities in the bank, which with increment amounted to about $2000. On the advice of his attorney the service of summons on Dunham was defective. He contended that notice by publication was not legal, as it was not shown that Dunham was out of the state and moreover that it was taken for granted that Dunham was alive when it could not be shown that he was alive or even outside of Santa Clara County, if not dead. Suit was then brought to force the Sheriff to sell the securities and apply the proceeds to the judgment, it being claimed that publication of summons was sufficient and that the Court could take sufficient knowledge of the acts of its own executive officers.

This morning Judge Kittredge handed down a decision sustaining the contention of Shesler and the Sheriff was ordered to sell the securities and apply the proceeds to the judgment. It is claimed that this is an entirely new case in California jurisprudence.

Newspaper: *San Francisco Chronicle*
Date: October 13, 1898

The mystery which has surrounded the disappearance of James C. Dunham, the San Jose murderer, has apparently been cleared away by the discovery of a skeleton in Lower California, fifteen miles from the eastern coast of the Gulf of California, midway between the ranch of Jose Murillo and the coast. J. A. Altamirano Jr., vice-president of the San Juan Mining Company, whose mines are at Los Flores, says that six weeks ago he went to the mines at Los Flores and from there to San Luis Rancho, about seventy miles northeast of the mines which ranch is owned by Jose Murillo, well and favorably known throughout that section.

Murillo seemed deeply concerned over a stranger whom he had fed and housed and who had suddenly disappeared. Some months afterward a skeleton was found fifteen miles from Murillo's ranch.

Murillo told Altamirano that in the middle of July, 1897, a man came to his house. As only criminals and hardened characters appear unattended upon lonely deserts in lower California, Murillo took particular notice of the stranger, who was dressed in a much-worn Prince Albert suit.

In appearance he seemed about 35 years old. He had greenish brown eyes, stood about five feet nine inches in height, wore a full reddish brown beard and had a profusion of brownish hair, which had not been trimmed for some time. He wore a black slouch hat and carried no weapons but had a small wicker-covered demijohn which he used for carrying water. One peculiarity Murillo observed was the wide space between two upper-front teeth when he spoke.

Murillo said that he engaged him in conversation on a variety of topics, but the stranger was evidently unwilling to converse. When fully rested the mysterious personage started west from San Luis Rancho toward the Gulf, thirty miles away, through one of the roughest, most dreary sections along the coast.

Two months ago Murillo and his hired men made a trip to the coast on business, and prospected some claims on the way. On the trip they found a skeleton and the belief that the bleached bones were the remains of the mysterious stranger were proved by the finding of the demijohn and portions of a Prince Albert coat. The skeleton is in a good state of preservation and shows two wide-apart teeth in the upper jaw. After the stranger had departed Murillo received from Guaymas officials a full description of the murderer Dunham, which had been sent to all parts of the country. Careful comparison between the man as he appeared at the ranch and the printed description fully convinced Murillo that he gave shelter to Dunham, and that he was probably the last man who saw Dunham alive.

Newspaper: *San Francisco Chronicle*
Date: December 29. 1898

COLUMBUS, OHIO - A man giving the name of Harry Church whom the police suspect of being James C. Dunham, the California murderer, has made the following statement:

> *I will plead guilty to being Dunham if they will pay about $10 I owe in this city and take my wife and me back to California where I want to go, for they will soon see there that I am not the man wanted and turn me loose in the place where I want to be. This is all nonsense. The police had better stop it as they are laughed at. Look at that picture and look at me. There is no similarity whatever. I knew Dunham and he killed someone, I believe. I'll admit the description looks suspicious but you can see that I am not the man.*

A stranger giving his name as Thomas Ward and claiming to be connected with a hotel in San Jose called at the City Prison to see Church last night. He said he knew Dunham well and that while Church answered the general description, he was not Dunham.

Church made an effort to get into court today, but will not have a hearing until tomorrow. He is held on a charge of vagrancy and will undoubtedly be sentenced to give further investigation. He said today that he had a wealthy sister in Sacramento, a Mrs. Bateman living on K. Street.

Newspaper: *San Francisco Chronicle*
Date: December 30. 1898

SACRAMENTO – The statement of Harry Church arrested in Columbus, Ohio, on suspicion of being James C. Dunham, that he has a wealthy sister in this city by the name of Mrs. Bateman is untrue. There is no such name as Bateman in the City Directory, nor is there such a name on the assessment roll. Direct inquiry this afternoon failed to locate any such person as the alleged Mrs. Bateman.

Newspaper: *San Francisco Chronicle*
Date: May 30, 1899

The Sheriff's office received a telegram this afternoon from Lampasas, Texas, asking if James C. Dunham is wanted here. As he is the fugitive slayer of the McGlincy family, an answer was sent saying that he is much wanted. The telegram is signed by "Rice King." No other facts are known.

Newspaper: *San Francisco Chronicle*
Date: August 15, 1899

It is a bitter blow to the detectives, but the suspect who has been under arrest here (Louisville, Kentucky) for the past nine days is evidently not James C. Dunham, the California murderer. The truth came out yesterday that the man in custody is C. F. Netterfield, just as he said he is. While the pictures of the men were startling alike and they had the same marks, scars, and little peculiarities, it seems clear that the man is from Ohio. A telegram from Chief Warren, Ohio, was received yesterday morning. It is as follows:

"Photo is that of C. F. Netterfield, who left here about 18 years ago."

Immediately on receipt of the telegram Netterfield was turned loose. He did not seem overjoyed at being released. In fact, he said he was rather sorry, for he wanted to be taken to California. He said he knew that when he reached that state it would soon be found that he was not the man wanted and they would have to release him. The people of California are noted for their sense of justice, and he believed that when the people heard of the hardships to which he had been exposed they would assist him to get a position. He realized that he was ruined, for it came out at the time he was arrested that he was a dope fiend of the worst type, and that he took thirty grains of the deadly drug every day.

Netterfield's case was a peculiar one. He was a decorative painter. Last May, in a spirit of bravado, he admits that he said while drinking in a saloon that he had a little boy somewhere in the west. He is said to have stated also that he was wanted in California for murder. Several times he conversed in German with the barkeeper, and also gave a good description of towns in California. Detective Armstrong was informed of the matter and sent to California for the names and descriptions of the different men wanted there for murder.

Newspaper: *San Francisco Chronicle*
Date: June 9, 1901

Ever since the atrocious murders, known as the Dunham murders, took place in Santa Clara County five years ago, arrests have been made in all parts of the country. Graphic dispatches have appeared in the papers claiming that the notorious murderer had been captured at last. According to these same dispatches he has been captured both dead and alive, in good health and in bad, sane and insane, prosperous and destitute.

Within the month we have once more been assured that "the only genuine" murderer Dunham has been captured. This time he has been captured in a tiny town in Kansas, whose only claims to distinction lie in having produced another "genuine" Dunham and in being a near neighbor to the town that Carrie Nation helped to make famous. He easily proved that he was somebody else.

Whether Dunham is ever found or not, the story of the murder will be told and retold for years to come. As long as stone endures, so long must the tale of the awful murders be told to those who read the strange inscription on the headstones of the murdered people who came to their deaths at the hands of James Dunham on May 27, 1896.

There is no prettier nor more peaceful cemetery in the land than the beautiful Oak Hill Cemetery in San Jose. Wide, winding driveways stretch and curve under the spreading shade trees. Huge oaks extend their gnarled limbs and graceful myrtles and elms mingle their branches overhead, and the quiet hills looking down protectively from the background, all go to make up what might be termed an ideal "City of Peace."

Bordering one of the main drives lies the plot in which are interred those five who met their untimely end at the hands of Dunham. The young wife of the murderer, her brother, the venerable master and mistress of the farm, the manservant—all lie side by side, the five innocent victims of a madman's bloody lust, each having merely a flat, white slab to mark his or her last resting place.

No distinction is made between the graves of the wealthy landowner and his wife and children and that of his humble servant. Each slab bears the name and age of the body it covers, and upon each slab is carved a word or two of the following quotation: "Vengeance is mine; I will repay, saith the Lord."

So they lie, master and man, side by side, and whoever conceived the idea of carving the simple, Scriptural text, did a thing, noble in its fine simplicity, utterly lacking in all base desires for revenge. What a pity similar inscriptions could not be placed on the graves of negroes, murdered at the hands of the mobs in the Bloody South.

It does not matter particularly whether Dunham is ever captured or not, for those who erected these stones believe that vengeance is meted out by a higher power than the hangman with his rope.

Newspaper: *San Francisco Chronicle*
Date: June 16, 1901

Three boys from East San Jose, ranging in age from 13 to 15, tired of the dull routine of school life, started out this morning for more thrilling adventures. One of their purposes, they announced to their fellows, was to track and catch the Campbell murderer, James C. Dunham. The boys were Charles Fisher and Ed and Willie Gruell. They were well-equipped for the trip. One of them stole his father's watch and bicycle and traded them for a donkey.

A cart was borrowed from a neighbor, and in this they loaded their baggage, which contained three axes, three hammers, a store of jam they had filched from the parental storehouse and two guns. The Sheriff was notified and caught the youthful adventurers a dozen miles from home, making lively tracks for the rising sun. They were brought back and turned over to their parents.

Newspaper: *San Francisco Chronicle*
Date: November 19. 1901

By a declaration rendered yesterday in the Supreme Court the aged parents of Minnie Shesler, one of the six victims of James C. Dunham, the Campbell murderer, will be deprived of $8000. This sum was awarded to them by the Superior Court of Santa Clara County, but now the judgment has been reversed on the ground of lack of jurisdiction.

Judge McFarland, in his concurring opinion, holds that "at the time of the institution of the action against Dunham and the rendition of the judgment he was a non-resident of this State, having neither his actual residence nor his legal domicile here."

As some people believe that Dunham died in the hills behind Mount Hamilton and others are sure that he escaped to some foreign land, there is little likelihood that the Sheslers will ever be able to get another judgment.

Newspaper: *San Francisco Chronicle*
Date: June 2, 1902

Another has been added to the list of victims of James C. Dunham—his own sister Alice. Just as surely as the death of the McGlincy family and their two employees was caused by the ax and gun which Jim Dunham wielded, the death of his sister has been caused by the remorse and sorrow that came to her as the result of that horrible tragedy. She changed her name from Dunham to Cobb by permission of the court to escape the stain on the family name. She traveled to other parts of the State with her changed name, but the story of her brother's crime followed her like a shadow. As her mind and will power weakened under the baleful influences, her body broke down under the strain, consumption set in and today she was laid at rest in the same cemetery where the six victims of her brother sleep under a single marble slab.

Some think she knew her brother's hiding place and the secret has borne her down to the grave.

There yet remains in the direct family Charles Cobb, a brother, and Dunham's own child, a baby in the cradle when its mother was killed.

The funeral was held quietly today from 164 East San Carlos Street, where she made her home since she became unable to work. She was

29 years of age. With her brother she was attending the State Normal School of this city at the time of the tragedy and graduated a year later. She taught at Hanford and Santa Ana and finally obtained a place in the San Francisco School Department last year. Whenever her identity was discovered she invariably lost her position. She possessed a loving and amiable disposition and had many genuine friends who sorrow at her premature and melancholy death.

Newspaper: *San Francisco Chronicle*
Date: September 3, 1904

In all probability another bogus Dunham has been arrested, this time at Naco, Arizona. The murderer of the McGlincy family near San Jose in 1896 had quite a number of impersonators. Since his disappearance from the scene of his crimes, persons suspected of being him have been arrested in Montana, Alabama, Iowa, Ohio, Kentucky, Indiana, Texas and Kansas. In some cases the description of the suspect has so closely tallied to that of Dunham that long distance trips have been made by Santa Clara County officers for the purpose of establishing the identity of the man under arrest and procuring his extradition. One suspect was actually brought to San Jose from Kansas before the authorities discovered that they had been fooled. Different accounts say that Dunham's skeleton has been found in lower California, he was killed by a Colorado sheriff at Meeker, he has been identified by officers incarcerated in a Mexican prison, he has been found reported as fighting with the Yaquis, and several times he has been found in Arizona where he has turned up once more.

In all of these instances, except the last named, the Dunham found has been proved to be either a case of mistaken identity or a fraud who was endeavoring to get a free ride to California or seeking to escape extradition to some other state, where he was really wanted to answer for some crime he had actually committed. But the real James C. Dunham is either still at large, or, what is more likely, has been long since dead.

(**Editor's note**: the following articles appeared after a series of photographs of a suspect were sent to the Santa Clara County Sheriff's Office.)

Newspaper: *San Jose Mercury*
Date: September 15, 1908

Has Jim Dunham, the most sought for murderer that ever committed a crime on the Pacific Coast, at last been captured? Law authorities are comparing new photographs to two existing photographs of Dunham.

The only real difference in the two faces is an expression of the eyes and the amount of flesh on the face. The eyes of the Dunham of twelve years ago are calm, steady eyes, the eyes of a man with a comparatively clear conscience. The eyes of the new suspect are the shifty eyes that mask many a guilty man's thoughts. The full face of the Dunham of twelve years ago is the face of a man who is not compelled to undergo any great amount of hardship to obtain the necessities and even the luxuries of life.

In the opinion of Deputy Sheriff Buffington, ex-jailer Byron Cottle and a few others who knew "Jim" Dunham intimately, the photograph of the suspect depicts Dunham as he would appear today, conscience-stricken, shifty-eyed, a dozen years older, worn in face and frame and with a face stamped by long watchfulness and ceaseless guarding against capture and punishment for his great crime.

The points of resemblance about the face are many and striking when the photographs are studied carefully. Cover up the eyes, and the noses, mouths and chins appear to have been cast in the same mold. Cut off a little of the flesh, and there are the same high cheekbones and the identical sweep of the jaw line. The ears are the same in outline. The foreheads are the same. The manner of wearing the hat is identical in each case.

With the photographs, which were received yesterday from Ex-Sheriff McAfee of Sherman, Texas, is the following letter giving a few additional details concerning the capture of the Dunham suspect:

Sheriff Langford, Sir:

Enclosed find photos of a man I think is J. C. Dunham. I have him in jail. He did not want to have his picture taken. He fills the description to a "T" except his hair is a little thin in front as you can see from the picture.

He came to this country on a Friday and met a widow woman, who had a small farm, and married her on the following Wednesday, which was the 9th day of July, 1908, and he began to try to sell the place the next week, but could make no title to the place.

He then tried to borrow money on the place and failed. She had a good team and wagon and he had fixed to leave with everything Saturday night but I arrested him that evening.

His wife is very glad we arrested him. She says she believes he was going to murder her and the children. He was very mad because she would not give him a bill of sale of the wagon and team.

Now if you have anybody who was well-acquainted with him I think they will know him by these photos. He claims he has been in Texas thirty years but cannot give me the name of anybody he knows or ever worked for in Texas. He wanted to know how many people were murdered there and if any of them was any relation to the man that murdered them.

Let me hear from you as early as possible as to what you think about him and if you are satisfied that he is your man what time can you get here to identify him?

R. L. McAfee, ex-Sheriff

Accompanying the letter are four pictures of the man who gives the name of Hatfield and claims to hail from Tennessee, but says that the greater part of the last thirty years has been in Texas. He cannot, however, give the names of any men he has worked for during all these years.

Since the information came to the office here, members of the Sheriff's force have been at work on the case at this end of the line, trying to find persons who were well acquainted with the criminal.

Of the several interviewed, almost without a moment's hesitation each one has declared the pictures shown to be excellent of the face and figure of the man wanted here.

Deputy Sheriff Howard "Buff" Buffington, who was talking with Dunham less than an hour before the tragedy was enacted, declares the pictures to be "dead ringers" of the murderer. It is very probable that a Deputy will be sent to Texas to bring the man to San Jose.

Newspaper: *San Jose Mercury*
Date: September 18, 1908

SHERMAN, TEXAS – Declaring that he is not James Dunham, wanted for the murder of six persons near San Jose, William Hatfield, who was placed in jail here on that charge, today issued a statement in which he asserts that he is a native of Tennessee, that he came to Texas when 16 years of age, has been in the State for the past 20 years, and has never been out of Texas since that time. He declares that he has worked in Texas as a farmhand, and that he never heard of the crime of Dunham until recently, when a similarity of appearance caused suspicions.

Evidence which every day seems more and more conclusive that the Hatfield man held by the authorities of Texas is the long-looked-for James C. Dunham is still being secured. For several days past the officer at Sherman and Sheriff Langford have been in communication, and the last piece of evidence, which seems almost incontrovertible that the suspect in Texas is the man wanted here, has been obtained.

In reply to a description of Dunham, sent by Sheriff Langford to Deputy U. S. Marshal McAfee in Sherman, Texas, the following message was received at the Sheriff's office yesterday morning:

(Hatfield) has bad scar on left foot. Get busy.

Dunham was well-marked in one particular. He carried a bad scar on the left foot, which he said he received from a careless use of an ax while chopping wood. This fact of the scar is one known to several persons connected with the case at the time the murder took place, and was also used on one occasion since, when Charles F. Crill, a Dunham suspect, was brought in by the officers of the county.

This fact of the scar was telegraphed to McAfee, who, after receiving the message had Hatfield remove his shoes and on the left foot was found a large scar, such as might be caused by an accident of character Dunham said he met with.

Sheriff Langford said yesterday: "It looks as though we have the man this time. There have been a good many wild-goose chases for former Dunham suspects, but the evidence which we have now certainly shows up all right. I have not been willing to do any more than make a careful investigation of the case, but this last piece of evidence seems so conclusive that immediate action will probably be taken to cause the man's return."

Late in the day a conference was held between the Sheriff and the District Attorney, who met to make arrangements for procuring the prisoner from Texas.

After a long conference it was decided that another message would be sent to Texas for additional descriptions of the prisoner, especially in regard to his height and weight. Another telegram to this effect was sent to Sherman last night. An answer is expected by wire this morning. If the height and weight correspond with the height and weight of Dunham, or if the height alone is within an inch of the height of Dunham, Sheriff Langford and Deputy Sheriff Buffington will leave at once to secure the prisoner, the last vestige of doubt removed from their minds that McAfee has the long-sought murderer.

The apparent cautiousness of the Sheriff is due to the many disappointments that the office has had in the past in going out of the State to identify Dunham suspects.

Considerable question has arisen concerning the possibility of obtaining evidence against the man who committed the murder more than twelve years ago, but it was learned at the Sheriff's office that a preponderance of evidence is still obtainable. Two men who witnessed the killing of two of the six persons murdered on May 26, 1896, by the murderous fiend are within the call of the authorities, and as soon as the man is identified will be subpoenaed as witnesses against him.

Newspaper: *San Jose Mercury*
Date: September 20, 1908

Mrs. Mary Zimmerman of San Francisco, formerly of San Jose, identified Hatfield as Dunham positively. Zimmerman had lived just a mile from the place where the wholesale slaughter took place. She did not want to go see Hatfield but eventually did.

Newspaper: *Campbell Interurban Press*
Date: September 23, 1908

Sheriff Langford and Deputy Buffington left Monday evening for Sherman, Texas, to bring home Hatfield, who is supposed to be

Dunham, the McGlincy murderer, and by the time this paper reaches our subscribers no doubt the facts will be known. "Buff" certainly ought to know him if anybody would.

Newspaper: *Campbell Interurban Press*
Date: September 23, 1908

Sheriff Langford and Deputy Howard Buffington are on their way back from Sherman, Texas, whither they went with requisition papers to bring Hatfield, the Dunham suspect.

He proved not to be the man though he bore a striking resemblance, and even "Buff" was kept guessing before he would give an answer as to whether it was Dunham or not. Thus another clue has gone glimmering.

Newspaper: *San Jose Mercury*
Date: September 24, 1908

On September 23rd, a telegram to the San Jose police chief from a Mrs. A. E. Davis of East Oakland pointed out that one discrepancy in the pictures that appeared in the *San Jose Mercury* that time cannot change; that is the lobe of the ear.

Newspaper: *Campbell Interurban Press*
Date: November 11, 1908

"Jim" Hatfield is now a free man, District Attorney Free making a motion to dismiss the charge. The matter came up before Judge Brown, Deputy Buffington having sworn to a complaint of murder. This was done simply to get the case before the court so that Hatfield could legally be dismissed. Out of some two dozen witnesses examined, there were none who would swear that the accused was Dunham, and practically all of them were decided in their opinion that Hatfield was not the man wanted.

Attorney Parker, of Fort Worth, Texas, happened to be going through San Jose and volunteered to defend Hatfield and he proved to be a popular and skilled attorney.

The courtroom was crowded to see and hear Hatfield testify. When Judge Brown dismissed the case Hatfield went up and shook the judge's hand and expressed his thanks. He says that the Santa Clara County officials have treated him well, but has much criticism for McAfee, as has also District Attorney Free, who says McAfee lied about the prisoner's physical appearance or else Hatfield wound not have been sent for.

The Jose Theater has engaged Hatfield for next week as a vaudeville star for those who want to pay to see the man who was not Dunham.

Editor's Epilogue

William Hatfield was the last suspect seriously thought to possibly have been James Dunham.

As time went on, the story of the sextuple murders would fade from the news and an influx of new residents to the thriving Santa Clara County, who were not present in 1896, most likely knew nothing of the story.

Historian Jeanette Watson recorded that Percy was raised by his great-aunt and great-uncle Brewer. If Dunham's commonly-believed motive was true, he was successful: Percy inherited the Campbell house and all of its belongings, although the child would never actually live there.

In January of 1906, when Percy was nine years old, his guardians put the house, horses, land, and the farm equipment up for sale, but there were no takers. The property was again offered for sale in August of that year (minus the horses, which had presumably sold in the interim), and successfully sold. The McGlincy house would stand for another 49 years, before finally being demolished in 1955 to make way for new buildings.

Local landmarks still exist, however. McGlincy Lane runs through a section of Campbell near the former homestead, and the local lodge of the International Order of Odd Fellows was named for Ada in 1897.

One big question remains: what was young Percy told about the gruesome night when he was only three weeks old? Never knowing any family other than the Brewers, some have speculated that he was completely spared the details of the horrible crime at the hands of his father and was told that Michael and Lucy Brewer were his natural parents.

Trace evidence proves he was told *something*, however. In 1956, when 60-year-old Florida resident Percy O. Brewer applied for a social security number, he did list his great-uncle Michael T. Brewer as his father, but listed his mother as "Hattie Wells."

APPENDIX ONE

Coroner's Inquiry Testimony of McGlincy neighbor L. C. Ross (excerpts)

L. C. Ross was sworn in and examined by District Attorney H. L. Partridge.

Q: Where do you reside Mr. Ross?

A: About 300 yards from here.

Q: You are the son of Daniel Ross?

A: Yes, sir.

Q: Were you home last night, the 26th day of May, 1896?

A: I got home about 9:15 o'clock.

Q: What time did you go to bed?

A: Ten o'clock or pretty sharp five minutes afterward.

Q: Did you go to sleep immediately?

A: No, sir.

Q: Did you read for a while?

A: Yes, sir.

Q: How long did you read?

A: I hardly know the exact time. Probably three-quarters of an hour or so.

Q: Your room is upstairs in the house?

A: Yes, sir.

Q: Is there a window in your room looking toward the McGlincy house?

A: Yes, sir, facing it.

Q: Was it up or down?

A: It was a half window and it was open.

Q: You read for three-quarters of an hour? About 10:45 you stopped reading and put out your light and went to bed?

A: I was in bed, yes, sir, and put out the light.

Q: Did you go to sleep?

A: No, sir.

Q: How long did you remain awake before going to sleep?

A: I hardly know. I had not gone to sleep up to the time I was roused out of bed. I should judge about half an hour.

Q: What aroused you?

A: It sounded to me like a pistol shot, and I got out and came to the back window. I thought all I heard was the windmill; it was not greased, and I thought it was the sound I heard. I went to bed and in about two minutes I heard a man screaming "Murder, help, he is killing me!"

Q: Did you recognize the voice?

A: Mr. McGlincy's.

Q: When you heard the cry what did you do?

A: I came downstairs as fast as I could, without much clothing.

Q: Did you dress at all?

A: A pair of overalls.

Q: You came downstairs running?

A: Yes, sir.

Q: And then went where?

A: My father stopped me at the foot of the stairs and asked where I was going. I told him there was trouble down here, and I thought it was murder, and I thought there might be some shooting. McGlincy's voice frightened me. I ran down the east side of the irrigation ditch and came out to the right, where the date palm stands.

Q: The one nearest the ditch?

A: Yes, sir.

Q: It was a bright moonlit night?

A: Yes, sir.

Q: You could see distinctly?

A: Yes, sir.

Q: You came down to the date palm. Did you hear any shooting?

A: Yes, sir, I heard two or three shots and heard a man say, "Don't shoot me, Jim, don't shoot me."

Q: They were running in what direction at that time?

A: I did not see them running. I heard them shooting a good way from me, and I could not see him going into the cabin.

Q: You saw who going into what cabin?

A: Afterwards it proved to be McGlincy

Q: The little cabin was where the hired men slept?

A: Yes, sir.

Q: You walked out to this date palm and stood in the shadow of that?

A: Yes, sir.

Q: You could see distinctly between yourself and the cabin?

A: Almost every motion.

Q: Could you see the front of the barn?

A: Everything distinctly.

Q: Did you notice whether or not the door upstairs in the barn was open?

A: I did not notice that.

Q: You stood there for how long?

A: I could not positively state. It was rather exciting. It might be one minute and a half or two minutes. I couldn't say.

Q: You saw McGlincy go into the cabin?

A: Yes, sir.

Q: Was he screaming as he was running?

A: No, sir; at that time he was not saying anything.

Q: This other party you assumed was Mr. Dunham?

A: Yes, sir.

Q: How far was Dunham behind him?

A: Not over twenty feet.

Q: Did you see him shoot then?

A: I heard the shots before and after I came.

Q: When McGlincy went in the cabin did he close the door?

A: Yes, sir; I could see that.

Q: What was the other party doing then?

A: Dunham? He shot one shot and stepped on the porch and looked as though he was loading his revolver, and I heard him say "Come on out."

Q: You recognized the voice?

A: Yes, sir; I would recognize it in a thousand voices. And I heard McGlincy say "No, sir. I have got two bullets in my body; I do not want to come out." And Dunham says "Come out. I want you," and he fired three or four times, and every time he shot McGlincy would moan, and afterwards McGlincy came out and Dunham stood there and shot.

Q: How many times?

A: Three or four times.

Q: What direction did he go?

A: Toward the house in kind of a circle. Dunham stood almost in front of the porch.

Q: And McGlincy ran in a circle in a direction toward the house?

A: Yes, sir, he endeavored to come this way and then back again.

Q: After McGlincy fell, Dunham walked up and shot two shots in his body?

A: Yes, sir.

Q: You were standing in the shadow of the palm?

A: Yes, sir, I did not move.

Q: Did you know anything in reference to the shooting of the hired man?

A: I did not see him come out of the cabin.

Q: After McGlincy was shot, did you see Dunham go to the rear of the cabin?

A: Dunham says, "I want George. I want them all." He hollered "George" several times. He walked to the rear of the cabin and there appeared to be a scramble. Dunham jumped into the house and came into the other room and then I started for him.

Q: You heard a crash at the rear of the house?

A: No, sir, I could not swear to it.

Q: Did you see Dunham go back to the house and stop?

A: No, sir, when I left he was still in the little cabin.

Q: How long did he remain in the cabin?

A: That I could not say. He was there when I left.

Q: You went back to your house and got your shotgun?

A: Yes, sir.

Q: After you went back to your house you notified your father?

A: Yes, sir.

Q: Where did you go then?

A: To Mr. Page's and woke him up and Mr. Whipple's and woke him up.

Q: How far is it from your house to Page's?

A: About 150 yards.

Q: How far from Mr. Whipple's?

A: Four or five hundred yards.

Q: You got them both out and waited?

A: I did not wait for Mr. Page; I went up and called him and called for Whipple and waited for him about two minutes; not longer than that.

Q: Then you came right here?

A: Yes, sir, to this place.

Q: Did you come to the main house before you found the body of the hired man?

A: Yes, sir.

Q: Did you come through and go through the house?

A: Yes, sir.

Q: Which door did you come in?

A: The side entrance.

Q: The back parlor?

A: Yes, sir.

Q: Was it opened or closed?

A: It was closed.

Q: Was there any light in the house?

A: No, sir, none except the lantern with us.

Q: The first body you found was that of James Wells?

A: Yes, sir.

Q: His clothes were on fire?

A: Yes, sir.

Q: Whom did you find when you arrived?

A: Nobody when we came; nobody; this George Schaible had gone up to my house and he came down with me.

Q: Did Page and your father come afterward?

A: Yes, sir; Page and Whipple were with me.

Q: When you left the main house did you then go immediately to the cabin?

A: Yes, sir.

Q: Did you find the body of McGlincy?

A: Yes, sir.

Q: Was he dead?

A: Yes, sir.

Q: Where was he?

A: Lying in front of the cabin facing this way; I should judge thirty feet.

Q: Then did you make any search for any other body?

A: I took a lantern and came out and saddled the horse, and Page went to the telephone station to call a doctor, and then we came to the main house to investigate.

Q: James Wells' clothes were on fire?

A: Yes, sir.

Q: Where was he lying?

A: Right in front of the fireplace, in the back parlor, just as he lays now.

Q: Did you discover the ax?

A: Yes, sir, lying within two feet of his head.

Q: Was the ax bloody?

A: Yes, sir.

Q: Did you examine him to see whether or not he was dead?

A: Yes, sir.

Q: He was dead?

A: Yes, sir.

Q: What did you do next?

A: We went into the dining room, and from there in the next room adjoining, we saw the mother.

Q: What was the state of the dining room?

A: Badly disordered; dishes broken and everything on the floor.

Q: In regard to the body of Mr. Wells, he was fully dressed?

A: Yes, sir.

Q: Did you notice any cut?

A: I did not know whether he was cut or not, indeed; the wounds, though, were powder burned.

Q: The floor had broken dishes and the tablecloth on it?

A: Yes, sir, and footprints as though it had been tramped.

Q: You discovered the body of Mrs. McGlincy next?

A: Yes, sir.

Q: Where was it?

A: Lying between the door and the bed.

Q: In her night clothes?

A: Yes, sir.

Q: Feet bare?

A: Yes, sir.

Q: Did you examine her to see whether or not she was alive?

A: Yes, sir. She was dead, quite cold.

Q: Did you notice any marks of violence upon her?

A: Yes, sir, it looked as though there was a stroke of the back of an ax breaking her skull clear into her eye.

Q: Then where did you go?

A: From there we went up the stairs.

Q: And discovered the body of whom?

A: The servant girl, Minnie Shesler.

Q: She was partially dressed? Had a wrapper on?

A: Yes, sir.

Q: Her feet were bare?

A: Yes, sir.

Q: She was in Mrs. Dunham's bedroom?

A: Yes, sir.

Q: Did you know the room Miss Shesler occupied?

A: I believe from what the hired man said she occupied the bedroom at the east side of the house.

Q: She was lying between the two beds in Mrs. Dunham's bedroom, nearest the door?

A: Yes, sir.

Q: Did you make any other discovery of any other body in the room at that time?

A: No, sir.

Q: Did you notice the clothes of the cot were piled up?

A: It looked as though somebody had just got out of bed. We looked under the bed and through the closets and found nothing.

Q: You came downstairs?

A: Yes, sir. We went through the cellar, kitchen and closets.

Q: Did you notice any blood in the kitchen?

A: No, sir.

Q: Did you notice the window open?

A: No, sir.

Q: When did you discover it open?

A: This morning. I found blood on the sill and sash.

Q: And a few drops of blood on the floor?

A: Yes, sir.

Q: You came down and went through the house and discovered nothing further?

A: Nothing, except what was found by finding her body later on.

Q: Whose body?

A: Mrs. Dunham's body.

Q: In regard to the body of Mr. Briscoe, he was found after you entered the house?

A: I think we discovered him afterward.

Q: You went through the house after the doctor came?

A: Yes, sir.

Q: You didn't discover the body of Mrs. Dunham until after the doctor came?

A: No, sir.

Q: You didn't discover the body of Mr. Briscoe before the doctor came?

A: I think the doctor was there; Mr. Schaible found him.

Q: You remained around the premises?

A: Waiting for the doctor; yes, sir.

Q: Mr. Page had gone for the doctor?

A: Yes, sir; went for the doctor and telephoned for the officers.

Q: He came back with a doctor?

A: No, sir, he did not, sir.

Q: Was Mr. Page with you?

A: I don't remember whether he was with us the first time or not; he was in at one time.

Q: You remember George Schaible was with you at some point?

A: Yes, sir.

Q: And went away on horseback?

A: He went to Mr. Wade's—to the telegraph office to telegraph San Francisco and did not have any success and came back.

Q: You don't know whether it was after the doctor arrived that you found the body of Briscoe?

A: No, sir; I would not be positive.

Q: Where was Briscoe's body found?

A: About six or seven rods from the cabin.

Q: Was he dead when you discovered him?

A: Yes, sir.

Q: About what time did you find his body?

A: About 12:45 o'clock.

Q: When Dr. Cooper arrived, you came back to the main house and went through the house again and found Mrs. Dunham?

A: Yes, sir. I found the little baby laying in his bed. I said Mrs. Dunham was here someplace, and at that time somebody discovered her foot and they said: "She is here."

Q: The clothes were piled over her completely?

A: Yes, sir; she lay on the cot sunken down in the clothes and we didn't notice her at all at the time.

Q: You have remained here almost constantly ever since that time?

A: Yes, sir; ever since.

Q: Did you know James Dunham?

A: Yes, sir.

Q: Did you know him pretty well?

A: I considered myself very well acquainted with him.

Q: You couldn't be mistake in regard to the man you saw being James Dunham?

A: No, sir, I could not.

Q: You recognized the name of McGlincy when he called him?

A: Yes, sir, and the name of Jim that McGlincy called him.

Q: Did you see a revolver in his hand?

A: Yes, sir, one in each hand. He shot with both hands. He would shoot with one and then the other.

Q: Do you know anything in reference to any trouble that has been here at the house before this?

A: I don't know anything serious that would cause a man to commit a crime like that.

Q: Did you know of any trouble?

A: There was an ill feeling between James Wells and Dunham before the marriage of his sister and ever since.

Q: Do you know whether there was trouble between Mr. and Mrs. Dunham?

A: I don't know.

Q: Do you know whether there had been any trouble between Dunham and McGlincy?

A: Nothing but an assertion that was made. There was talk here at one time, and McGlincy didn't believe it.

Q: It was in regard to the $1000?

A: Yes, sir.

Q: Dunham claimed he was robbed of $1000 he took from the bank and that he bought two bicycles?

A: Yes, sir.

Q: McGlincy didn't believe that?

A: No, sir.

Q: There was no serious trouble?

A: Nothing but warm words.

Q: How long ago was that?

A: About two months ago.

Q: The baby was three weeks old?

A: Yes, sir.

Q: This situation with the $1000 happened about four or five weeks before the birth of the baby?

A: It was something like that; about six weeks or two months. I don't remember.

Q: Whose money was this?

A: He claimed it was his own—Dunham's money.

Q: Do you know anything in relation to the religion of the family?

A: As far as religion is concerned, I don't think any of them were members of any church. Mrs. McGlincy was inclined toward the church a great deal. I don't remember whether she was a member or not. The men—all three—were members of the A.P.A.

Q: Reputed members?

A: Yes, sir, they wore the badges.

Q: All three of them?

A: Yes, sir.

Q: Mr. Dunham as well as McGlincy and his son, Mr. Wells?

A: Yes, sir.

Q: Do you know anything in regard to the religious opinions of Mrs. Dunham?

A: I do not; I have never heard her mention anything at all.

Q: Was Mrs. Dunham rather of an excitable nature?

A: No, sir; very cool-headed. I have seen her under trying circumstances once.

Q: How long ago was that?

A: Something over five or six months before her marriage. The house got a fire and she was perfectly cool and calm at the time.

Q: She and Mr. Dunham were married how long?

A: I think some time in December a year ago.

Q: December of 1894?

A: Yes, sir; 1894 I think.

Q: Do you know whether Dunham was in poor circumstances financially?

A: I heard he had an estate left him over a year ago—a short time before he was married, whether he had it or not I couldn't say.

Q: Do you know anything in regard to Dunham's habits; whether he gambled or not?

A: No, sir; nobody thought that here.

Q: Did he drink?

A: I never heard it.

Q: How old a man was he?

A: 27 or 28. I think he was 28 years old.

Q: Had he a violent temper?

A: Always very mild in conversation and general manners.

Q: When you found the body of the servant girl upstairs, did you notice whether or not there was a gag in her mouth?

A: Yes, sir.

Q: What was it?

A: It looked to me like torn clothes, strips two or three or four inches wide at the corners and then big pieces.

Q: In the mouth of Mrs. Dunham was there also a gag?

A: Yes, sir.

Q: Who removed the gag?

A: Dr. Cooper.

Q: The gag in Mrs. Dunham's mouth was also of the same kind?

A: A little larger, if anything.

Q: In relation to the revolver, did you see the revolver here on the step?

A: Yes, sir.

Q: Did you examine it?

A: Yes, sir.

Q: Where did you find it?

A: On the left-hand side of the porch as you go down. Barrel pointing outward at full cock, one chamber loaded, the rest empty.

Q: Empty? Empty shells in it?

A: I didn't examine it for that.

Q: Could you tell whether it was recently discharged?

A: I couldn't tell that. We gave it to Sheriff Lyndon and he drew a diagram of the porch where it lay.

Q: About what size was it?

A: And old-fashioned .45 Colt; a rim fire, from the looks of the handle.

Q: When did you discover it?

A: Somewhere about 2 o'clock. After we discovered all the bodies. Going around the house we discovered the revolver on that step there.

END

APPENDIX TWO

Coroner's Inquire Testimony of George Schaible (excerpts)

George Schaible was sworn in and examined by District Attorney H. L. Partridge.

Q: You reside here on the McGlincy ranch?

A: Yes, sir.

Q: How long have you worked here?

A: Since the 23rd of January, 1896.

Q: You worked here once before that, did you not?

A: Yes, sir.

Q: How long did you work here before?

A: About seven months.

Q: That was prior to the marriage of Dunham and Miss Wells?

A: Yes, sir.

Q: Do you know anything in relation to any trouble in the family?

A: Nothing but what Mr. McGlincy told me.

Q: You know nothing of your own knowledge?

A: No, sir.

Q: Do you know anything in relation to the threatened lawsuit of Mr. Dunham against Mr. McGlincy?

A: Nothing but what Mr. McGlincy told me.

Q: What did he tell you?

A: He told me that James Dunham was going to sue him last year for injuries he received two years ago.

Q: From falling off a ladder?

A: Yes, sir.

Q: Do you know anything in regard to the claim of Dunham being robbed of $1000?

A: Yes, sir; he made such a claim to his wife.

Q: How long before the birth of the baby?

A: About a month; I don't know exactly.

Q: Do you know whether or not Mr. McGlincy believed that or not?

A: He didn't believe it.

Q: How do you know that?

A: He told me so.

Q: Could you distinguish the voice you heard screaming for help?

A: I think it was McGlincy. I heard the shots fired again, about three or four. Then I heard them screaming again, and after that Mr. McGlincy came running out here.

Q: When Mr. McGlincy came running out, did he come around the corner of the main house or out of this door?

A: I couldn't tell.

Q: Before you saw him running around the corner, did you hear any crash?

A: No sir; then he ran towards the barn and called me and the boys.

Q: Did he have anything in his hand?

A: I didn't see anything. The he ran in the cabin, and Briscoe started to talk to him, and I saw Dunham coming out through the front door.

Q: At this time you were standing at the west end of the barn?

A: Yes, sir.

Q: How far behind McGlincy was Dunham?

A: McGlincy got pretty near to the corner of the barn before Dunham came out.

Q: Was Mr. McGlincy calling?

A: Yes, sir, he called, "George, George, George!"

Q: Did he say anything about being murdered?

A: No, sir. Then I saw Dunham coming and I went upstairs in the barn.

Q: Did you notice whether or not Dunham had anything in his hands?

A: No, sir.

Q: Were you still at the west end of the barn?

A: No, sir; I went up in the barn.

Q: You had changed from the west end of the barn to the east end of the barn and went in the east door, did you?

A: No, sir. I went through the window.

Q: You didn't come around through the east end at all?

A: No, sir.

Q: You were standing at the west end and you passed over from the west end of the barn to this window; you went by the north side of the barn?

A: Yes, sir.

Q: The barn was between you and the main house?

A: Yes, sir.

Q: How long did it take you to go from the west end of the barn where you could see Mr. McGlincy come out and Mr. Dunham, from that point to the doorway upstairs in the barn—how long did it take you to go there?

A: About a minute.

Q: Did you go immediately to that door you had opened?

A: No, sir; I waited a little while.

Q: At the bottom or the top of the stairs?

A: At the top of the stairs.

Q: There is a stairway that runs to the loft?

A: Yes, sir.

Q: When you got to the doorway, did you stand in full view or peek around the edge of the door?

A: I peeked around the edge of it.

Q: From where you stood could you see the cabin?

A: Yes, sir.

Q: In plain view?

A: There were some limbs in front of it.

Q: Where was Mr. McGlincy when you got to the door?

A: Inside the cabin.

Q: This talking you heard, was it the time when you changed your position?

A: Yes, sir; the talk was in the cabin.

Q: Where was Mr. Dunham?

A: Outside of the cabin.

Q: Did you notice whether or not he had any weapons?

A: I couldn't tell.

Q: Did he do any talking?

A: Not right away.

Q: Did he go to the door of the cabin?

A: No, sir.

Q: Why didn't he go in?

A: He couldn't get in.

Q: The door was secured in some way?

A: Yes, sir.

Q: This door has an ordinary lock?

A: Yes, sir.

Q: This door is off one of its hinges?

A: Yes, sir; it was not before; it is now.

Q: It was all right when you went away last night to Campbell?

A: Yes, sir.

Q: Dunham tried the door and tried to get in?

A: Yes, sir.

Q: Did he say anything?

A: Not right away.

Q: Did he after a while?

A: He walked around the cabin and went behind and fired three or four shots behind the cabin.

Q: Passed out of sight?

A: Yes, sir.

Q: How long did he remain there out of sight?

A: Perhaps a minute.

Q: And Mr. McGlincy remained inside the cabin?

A: Yes, sir.

Q: Did you hear any crash or anything before these shots?

A: No, sir.

Q: Did you hear any noise like a person going through the window?

A: No, sir.

Q: And he remained about a minute in the rear of the cabin?

A: Yes, sir.

Q: He came around front again?

A: Yes, sir.

Q: Mr. McGlincy was in the cabin?

A: Yes, sir.

Q: Did Dunham say anything?

A: Yes, sir.

Q: What did he say?

A: He walked up to the door and called, "Mac, come out, I want you," and Mr. McGlincy said he wouldn't go out. He said he was shot and had two bullets in his body already and couldn't go out, and Dunham called him again and he wouldn't come out and Dunham fired three or four shots.

Q: Do you know whether or not there was any coolness or apparent ill-feeling between Dunham and Mr. McGlincy?

A: Not that I know of.

Q: Did you notice anything that led you to believe there was any trouble?

A: No, sir.

Q: You need to come to the main house and spend the evening occasionally?

A: Yes, sir.

Q: And play cards with Dunham and McGlincy?

A: Yes, sir.

Q: How long did that continue?

A: Two or three weeks.

Q: Every night?

A: Yes, sir.

Q: It stopped suddenly?

A: Yes, sir.

Q: Do you know the cause of it?

A: No, sir.

Q: Before that time had there been friendship between Mr. McGlincy and Dunham?

A: Yes, sir.

Q: After that, how was it?

A: They never spoke to each other after that.

Q: Before that they talked together frequently?

A: Yes, sir.

Q: You didn't know the cause?

A: No, sir.

Q: That was before the pretended loss of the $1000?

A: Yes, sir.

Q: You were in Campbell last night?

A: Yes, sir.

Q: What time did you go there?

A: About half past 8:00.

Q: Did you leave at the same time McGlincy and Wells did?

A: Yes, sir.

Q: Did you remain with them all the time after that in Campbell?

A: Yes, sir.

Q: They went in a buggy?

A: Yes, all three in the buggy.

Q: What time did you leave Campbell?

A: About 11:00.

Q: And drove home all three together?

A: Yes, sir. Drove home pretty fast.

Q: Where did you usually sleep?

A: In the cabin.

Q: Where Mr. Briscoe did?

A: Yes, sir.

Q: How long has Mr. Briscoe worked there?

A: About three months.

Q: Did you know him before he worked there?

A: No, sir.

Q: How old was he?

A: Thirty years.

Q: How do you know that?

A: He told me so.

Q: In this cabin there are two rooms and a cupboard?

A: Yes, sir.

Q: The front room is larger?

A: Yes, sir.

Q: There is a bed in the front room?

A: Yes, sir.

Q: Who slept there?

A: Briscoe.

Q: There was a bed in the small room?

A: Yes, sir.

Q: Who slept there?

A: I did.

Q: In the rear of the cabin there is a window?

A: Yes, sir.

Q: An ordinary sized window?

A: Yes, sir.

Q: You could recognize Dunham when he came out of the front door of the main house?

A: Yes, sir.

Q: Recognized his voice?

A: Yes, sir.

Q: Told by his looks he was Dunham?

A: Yes, sir.

Q: Did Mr. McGlincy call him by name?

A: Yes, sir.

Q: Called him what?

A: Jim.

Q: That is the way Mr. McGlincy called him?

A: Yes, sir.

Q: Dunham fired two or three shots?

A: Yes, sir.

Q: At what?

A: Right through the door.

Q: Did you notice whether or not the door opened at all?

A: Not that I could see.

Q: Do you know whether the door at any time was slightly opened?

A: No, sir.

Q: How long did McGlincy remain in the cabin without coming out—before he finally came out?

A: Perhaps three minutes.

Q: In the meantime Dunham stood there, and then around in the rear about a minute, and came back to the front again?

A: Yes, sir.

Q: Did McGlincy come out finally?

A: Dunham told him to come out, and McGlincy told him to put his pistol away and he would come out.

Q: What did Dunham say to that?

A: He said, "All right, come on."

Q: Then did McGlincy open the door and come out?

A: Not right away, and finally he opened it and came out and I heard a crash just like someone was struck with something.

Q: Could you see anything take place at this time?

A: No, sir.

Q: Do you know whether Mr. McGlincy had anything in his hands or not?

A: I don't know.

Q: You say you heard a crash as though somebody was struck?

A: Yes, sir.

Q: Then what took place?

A: Then Mr. McGlincy ran past Dunham, and he fired two or three shots at him.

Q: What direction was McGlincy running at that time?

A: Running towards the main house.

Q: Where was Dunham standing?

A: On the porch of the cabin, and walked off while shooting; walked off in the direction of the barn.

Q: McGlincy ran in a direct line of the main house or in a circle?

A: After the shots he made a circle and fell.

Q: He was going in the direction of the main house when the shots were fired?

A: Yes, sir.

Q: How many were fired?

A: Two or three.

Q: Mr. Dunham was standing on the porch when he began to shoot, while he was firing these shots?

A: Yes, sir.

Q: How far did he walk while he was firing?

A: I couldn't tell.

Q: Sixteen feet?

A: Perhaps.

Q: Did he shoot him after he fell?

A: Yes, sir; twice after he fell.

Q: After McGlincy came, while he was running toward the main house, did he say anything then?

A: Yes, sir; yelled—yelled for help.

Q: Did he mention any names?

A: No, sir.

Q: Didn't he call for George or say anything about Jim?

A: No, sir.

Q: Then when Mr. McGlincy fell, you say Dunham advanced and fired two more shots at him?

A: Yes, sir.

Q: Stooped over?

A: Yes, sir, and fired in the body twice.

Q: Stooped over and deliberately fired twice?

A: Yes, sir.

Q: Did you observe how many weapons Dunham had?

A: No, sir.

Q: After Dunham shot McGlincy, what did he do?

A: Walked toward the cabin again.

Q: To go inside?

A: Not right away.

Q: How long did he stay around there?

A: Perhaps half a minute.

Q: Then he went inside, did he?

A: He called me.

Q: Called you?

A: Yes, sir; he called "George!"

Q: How many times did he call you?

A: Perhaps six different times.

Q: You didn't answer him?

A: No, sir.

Q: After he called you perhaps six different times, what did he do then?

A: He went around behind the back of the cabin and knocked the window in. I heard the crash of the window.

Q: You could hear the crash of the window after he went behind the cabin?

A: Yes, sir.

Q: Any shots fired then?

A: No, sir.

Q: Just before the shooting at the cabin, did you hear him call you before that?

A: No, sir.

Q: You didn't hear him call you?

A: No, sir.

Q: Did you hear anything, hear him say anything about he would "have to get all of them"?

A: I don't remember.

Q: He may have used that remark?

A: Yes, sir.

Q: If Mr. Ross heard it you wouldn't contradict it?

A: No, sir.

Q: You didn't hear it yourself?

A: No, sir.

Q: You heard him knock the window in?

A: Yes, sir.

Q: Do you know whether or not he went into the cabin after he knocked the window in?

A: I couldn't tell; he knocked the table over.

Q: Did you see him come out of the cabin?

A: He came around from the rear again.

Q: Did he remain there in front of the cabin for any length of time?

A: He walked up to the cabin door and called me again.

Q: Then he went inside?

A: Yes, sir.

Q: How long did he remain inside?

A: Not very long; perhaps half a minute.

Q: He came out of the front door?

A: Yes, sir.

Q: What did he do then?

A: Walked toward the orchard, where we found Briscoe.

Q: How long did he stay there?

A: He didn't stay there long; came right away.

Q: Did he walk up far enough to where Briscoe lay?

A: Yes, sir.

Q: Could you see him?

A: Yes, sir, but not very good.

Q: Could you see him down by the fence?

A: Yes, sir.

Q: Did you notice the spot?

A: Yes, sir.

Q: Could you say he went to where Briscoe's body was found?

A: I couldn't tell exactly.

Q: He stopped there?

A: Yes, sir.

Q: Did you see him stoop over?

A: No, sir.

Q: Did he fire any shots?

A: No, sir.

Q: Did you see Briscoe when he got out of the cabin and walked down there and how he got down there?

A: No, sir.

Q: You don't know at what time of the shooting Briscoe was killed?

A: No, sir.

Q: Dunham went afterwards to where you found Briscoe's body and remained there for a little while and came back?

A: Yes, sir.

Q: Then he stood around the cabin?

A: Yes, sir, and got his horse.

Q: The same one you had been driving?

A: Yes, sir.

Q: Put a bridle on it?

A: No, sir.

Q: Did he put a saddle on it?

A: No, sir, the saddle was there.

Q: Did you remain in the doorway upstairs?

A: I crawled off and lay in the middle of the floor.

Q: Did he strike a light downstairs?

A: Not at that time.

Q: He was in the barn and then went out again?

A: Yes, sir.

Q: Where did he go?

A: I don't know.

Q: How long was he gone?

A: Not very long, half a minute or a minute.

Q: Do you know where he went?

A: No, sir.

Q: Could you hear which direction he went?

A: No, sir.

Q: You don't know whether he came in the direction of the cabin?

A: No, sir.

Q: You don't know whether he went in the direction of the main house?

A: No, sir.

Q: Did you hear him go away from the barn at all?

A: I heard him go a few steps.

Q: Had he put the horse in the stall then?

A: No, sir.

Q: Where was the horse then?

A: In the barn.

Q: You say he was gone for half a minute or so?

A: Yes, sir.

Q: He came back again?

A: Yes, sir.

Q: The door was closed? When he went out he closed it?

A: Yes, sir.

Q: Did he call to you any more?

A: No, sir.

Q: When he came back the second time, what did he do?

A: Struck a match.

Q: Do you know for what purpose?

A: No, sir.

Q: Did he strike more than one?

A: No, sir.

Q: You were still lying upstairs on the floor?

A: Yes, sir.

Q: Do you know what he did then?

A: Took the horse out.

Q: Do you know whether he put a bridle or saddle on the horse?

A: I don't know.

Q: You know he didn't put a saddle on it?

A: Yes, sir.

Q: He led the horse out?

A: Yes, sir.

Q: Did you go to the door again?

A: I heard him gallop off on the horse. I got up and went to the other end of the barn.

Q: In what direction did he gallop?

A: Towards the main house.

Q: In this direction?

A: Yes, sir.

Q: To the north of the house?

A: Yes, sir.

Q: There are two entrances to this place?

A: Yes, sir.

Q: On entrances is from the Casey Road and the other from the Los Gatos Road?

A: Yes, sir.

Q: He went to the gate leading to the Casey Road?

A: Yes, sir.

Q: Did he go out through the gate?

A: No, sir.

Q: Stopped and got off the horse?

A: I couldn't tell; it was in the shadow.

Q: He was right here close to the main house?

A: Yes, sir.

Q: How long did he stay there?

A: A minute or two.

Q: You don't know whether he came inside of the house or not?

A: No, sir.

Q: He came out again?

A: Yes, sir.

Q: Got on his horse and rode in what direction?

A: Rode around the barn.

Q: Passing the west end or the east end of the barn?

A: The east end.

Q: You were standing by the west end of the door?

A: I moved from that end to the other.

Q: Did he run his horse out of here?

A: A slow gallop.

Q: What direction did he go then?

A: Toward the orchard.

Q: Toward the Los Gatos Road?

A: No, sir; down by the lane.

Q: Did he come back again?

A: Yes, sir.

Q: And then came back yet again?

A: Yes, sir.

Q: How long was he down that road?

A: Not very long; not more than a minute and a half.

Q: Then he came back to the yard again?

A: Yes, sir.

Q: What did he do then?

A: Went up the road.

Q: Toward the Los Gatos Road?

A: Yes, sir.

Q: That was the last time you saw him?

A: Yes, sir.

Q: Did you stay up in the barn?

A: Yes, sir.

Q: After he had gone down toward the Los Gatos Road on horseback, did you come down from the barn immediately?

A: Yes, sir.

Q: What did you do?

A: Went over to a neighbor's, Mr. Ross.

END

Made in the USA
Columbia, SC
28 June 2020